Fruitful

An Hachette UK company
www.hachette.co.uk

First published in Great Britain in 2024 by Kyle Books,
an imprint of Octopus Publishing Group Limited
Carmelite House, 50 Victoria Embankment
London EC4Y 0DZ
www.kylebooks.co.uk

ISBN: 978 1 80419 103 3

Distributed in the US by Hachette Book Group, 1290 Avenue
of the Americas, 4th and 5th Floors, New York, NY 10104

Distributed in Canada by Canadian Manda Group,
664 Annette St., Toronto, Ontario, Canada M6S 2C8

Additional photo credits: p. 67, © Giovanni and Asunta Bernabei; p. 89, © Sarah
Johnson; pp. 156–7 © David Mas Masumoto, photographed by Staci Valentine;
pp. 230–1, © Mags Coughlan. **Recipe credits:** pp. 133–4 Skye Gyngell

Publisher: Joanna Copestick
Editor: Isabel Jessop
Designer: Rachel Cross
Art Director: Jonathan Christie
Photographer: Patricia Niven
Food Stylists: Henrietta Clancy and Dor Harel
Prop Stylist: Rachel Vere
Location & Styling Direction: Lisa Gulick
Farm Location: Heckfield Home Farm
Production: Lucy Carter & Nic Jones

Printed and bound in China

10 9 8 7 6 5 4 3 2 1

Fruitful

Sweet and Savoury Fruit
Recipes Inspired by Farms,
Orchards and Gardens

Sarah Johnson
For Eleri and Ethan

KYLE BOOKS

Contents

Introduction

It all began with a fig. I remember strolling down a dappled lane towards my friend's organic farm in Northern California one late summer day. He had studied permaculture at university and was now devoted to growing nutritious food for the local community, using regenerative methods that improved the natural world around him. As we walked past a row of Meyer lemon trees that opened onto a field filled with vegetables and flowers, I noticed praying mantises and yellow-billed magpies, and the faint humming of bees could be heard all around. Surrounding the perimeter were impressive stalks of wild blossoming fennel and blackberry vines climbing into gnarled fig trees. We took refuge from the sweltering heat under the shade of one of the trees and gazed out onto the small farm. As I bit into the soft, syrupy fig, with its delicate skin and rich jammy texture, the connection between the vibrant land and the delicious food growing on it became clear. Even today, this is one of those memories that stresses its importance; we discover a lot about our food when we are more connected to the land where it is grown.

In recent times, more farmers have been moving away from intensive methods of farming in favour of practices that preserve the land and produce high-quality food. In homes and professional kitchens alike, cooks are increasingly seeking out more diverse ingredients. In an effort to find food that is fresher and more delicious, they are turning to farmers' markets, veg box schemes and even their own gardens. This newfound interest is encouraging more farmers to grow high-quality produce and bypass suppliers to sell their products directly to consumers. This book celebrates both the beauty and the bounty of fruit, as well as the farms, orchards and gardens that nurture them.

My cooking journey started at Alice Waters' Chez Panisse Restaurant in Berkeley, California, where I found myself nestled between boxes of freshly picked fruit. There were Kishu tangerines, Mara de Bois strawberries, and Suncrest peaches, and we could identify these fruits by their specific varieties because we worked closely with passionate farmers who grew for flavour, quality and diversity. Chez Panisse has always been an exemplary model of the farm-to-table movement. The relationships between the chefs and the farmers seemed to grow stronger every year and, through the restaurant, Alice proved that something as simple as eating was an agricultural act. These ethical principles grounded my work for years to come.

Eventually, I left behind my beloved home in California for London to work with Skye Gyngell at Spring Restaurant. Skye was joining forces with Fern Verrow Farm to bring fresh biodynamic produce to her restaurant in London. As the head pastry chef, I helped to foster the relationship between the kitchen and the farm. Working with Skye enabled me to expand the boundaries of my cooking, enhancing my creativity. Throughout the years, however, sourcing fresh ingredients and collaborating with farms have remained my primary focus. I helped to oversee the opening of Heckfield Place Hotel in Hampshire, England, and continue to collaborate with the growers of the on-site biodynamic market garden.

WHEN COOKING WITH FRUIT, LET SIMPLICITY BE YOUR GUIDE

Honest cooking begins with fresh, flavourful ingredients. It is easy to improve almost any dish by tasting the ingredients first. In the case of fruit, this means tasting for ripeness and flavour. In the opinion of a dear friend and sommelier, the best way to learn about wine is to drink it. It may seem that he is inviting us to drink wine to our hearts' content, however, he is merely conveying the importance of tasting and drinking wine repeatedly. This principle applies to food as well – tasting frequently and registering the taste in your mind is a meaningful lesson in becoming a good cook. By doing so, you awaken your senses to freshness and quality. I hope this book will serve as a guide in appreciating the flavours already present in the ingredients, so that they may be prepared using simple techniques.

What do we mean when we say that something tastes delicious? Experts in the field of wine discuss aroma, body, temperature, texture, acidity, and how they interact. I believe the same can also be applied to cooking with fruit (after all, isn't wine made from fruit?). By thinking critically about these characteristics, we can learn how to respond to them while cooking.

I have given measurements in the recipes when I believe they are essential. However, the amounts of salt, pepper, olive oil, acidity and even sugar may be determined by the varying flavour of the other ingredients. Not to mention your own personal preferences. Therefore, I encourage you to taste and discover how fruit changes with the seasons, as well as how it is altered by cooking. These little lessons will build your confidence in the kitchen and over time your reliance on recipes will fade as your intuition grows.

HOW TO USE THIS BOOK

A NOTE ON INGREDIENTS

Fruit: All the fruit in this book is intended to be ripe and eaten in season. Fruit should be fragrant and heavy in the hand. Berries will be coloured all the way through, and stone fruits will give slightly when pressed near the stem. Stems and leaves are also good indicators of freshness, so look for those that are green and supple.

Vegetables, dairy and eggs: Vegetables are also in tune with the season. Milk is whole and cream is always double cream, suitable for whipping. Eggs are fresh, medium in size, and come from pastured chickens raised on farms that maintain high standards of animal welfare.

Meat, poultry and seafood: Animals that are farmed in harmony with nature are often healthier and produce better-tasting meat. Well-raised meat and poultry command a higher price, but it is worth paying what you can afford. Fish and shellfish should be fresh, from sustainable populations, and be wild-caught from fisheries or fishermen using environmentally responsible practices.

A NOTE ON EQUIPMENT

As someone who likes to cook, I take a lot of pleasure in cooking with my hands. My hands tear open ripe persimmons, pluck fresh herbs from their stems and massage vanilla seeds into sugar. I can gauge the ripeness of a peach or determine if strawberries are room temperature. With that said, there are a few basic pieces of equipment that I find useful to have in the kitchen. It will also help to read the recipe through before you begin. Well-made equipment

and utensils increase the joy of cooking. If you're someone who regularly indulges in cooking or baking, chances are you already have most of the equipment needed for the recipes in this book. Here's the equipment I used to bring these recipes to life:

Fruit cutting board: Find a cutting board that is exclusively used for slicing fruit. A small wooden cutting board is easily affordable and takes up little space in the kitchen. It prevents fruit from mingling with undesirable flavours like onions or garlic, and is a simple way to improve your enjoyment of fruit.

Kitchen scales: For the best, most consistent results when following the recipes in this book, use kitchen scales and measure the ingredients in grams.

Sharp knives: Most cooking can be done with a sturdy, sharp chef's knife and a small well-made paring knife. A bread knife is also handy. When working with fruit, a tourné (or bird's beak) knife is useful for hulling strawberries or removing cores. Personally, I find a small serrated paring knife ideal for slicing through stone fruit, or fibrous rhubarb. Higher quality knives are sturdier and will keep a sharp edge for longer. Thankfully, nowadays there are numerous cost-effective options that provide excellent quality. Keeping your knives sharp is essential for supreming citrus, as well as chopping vegetables and trimming meat. Fresh herbs also stay fresher when chopped with a well-honed blade.

Ovenproof casserole: This is the preferred dish for Braised Pork Shoulder with Cider and Caramelized Apples (page 217) or North African Scented Lamb with Plums (page 176). It is also great for making jams and marmalades, cooking large stone fruits into purées (page 15), and poaching fruit (page 26).

Cast-iron pan: I use a shallow 23cm (9in) pan for most of my daily cooking. It's perfect for Pan-fried Duck Breast (page 86), Mackerel (page 92), Caramelized Apples (page 215) or Buckwheat Crêpes (page 225). If you don't have a cast-iron pan, then use a heavy-bottomed stainless steel or enamelled pan.

Ceramic roasting tray: For all your roasted fruit needs. Most of the recipes in this book were tested using a 20–22cm (8–8½in) ceramic roasting tray.

Food processor and blender: I do love the efficiency of a well-made food processor and blender. I use the food processor to blitz berries for sorbet, or even mix nut-based cakes. The Almond Cake with Greengages and Fennel Cream (page 175), Hazelnut and Pear Cake with Espresso (page 228) and Almond Marmalade Cake (page 60) all come together easily in a food processor. I reserve the powerful blender for blending the Delicata Soup with Apples, Brown Butter and Fried Sage (page 209), making Mint Ice Cream (page 105) and even mixing the Ginger Cake (page 90).

Stand mixer or electric whisk: This is used for sabayons, semifreddos, Swiss meringues and the Coconut Rum Cake (page 161).

Ice-cream maker: Store-bought ice cream, including many artisanal brands, often contains added emulsifiers and preservatives. By making ice cream at home, you can avoid these additives, and control the amount of sugar. It's also a great way of showcasing ripe fruit at the peak of its season.

Bowl, whisk, spatula and wooden spoon: Most of the recipes in this book can be made by simply using a bowl, whisk, spatula and wooden spoon. You'll find them useful for making salads, vinaigrettes, sauces and mayonnaise. A large bowl is handy when straining cooked fruit, cooling an ice-cream base or mixing mincemeat.

IN THE WORDS OF THE FARMER

Throughout the book you will find passages written by farmers who share their stories and thoughts on what it takes to grow delicious, quality fruit. We rely on farmers to create the optimal growing conditions for nutritious, flavourful produce, to know when to harvest it at peak ripeness and how to preserve its integrity during transport. When writing about fruit, I felt the story was incomplete if I alone tell it. The farmers' thoughts and observations connect us more deeply to the food we love.

FLAVOUR CHARTS

Every fruit section is accompanied by a chart that suggests how the fruit may be paired with various flavours. One of the greatest joys of cooking is that of discovery. These flavour charts are intended to arouse your own creativity and encourage you to adapt recipes or develop new dishes of your own. You may prefer to cook with flavours that you feel are underrepresented in these charts or find that some of the pairings do not suit your personal tastes. In that case, I hope you will be inspired to create your own flavour pairings, and from there expand your creativity.

TECHNIQUES FOR COOKING WITH FRUIT

Purées for Sauces, Ice Creams and Sorbets

Fruit purées are a valuable ingredient to have in the kitchen. They serve as a base for both savoury or sweet sauces, and can be transformed into ice creams and sorbets. They also make nice additions to vinaigrettes or cordials. Purées come to the rescue when you have soft, slightly damaged, or overripe fruit that you don't want to go to waste. As long as the fruit itself tastes good, the resulting purée will taste equally delicious. The techniques used to transform a whole fruit into a purée will greatly impact the flavour and texture of the final product, and vary depending on the fruit. Most fruit will fall into two categories: what I refer to as no-heat purées and flash-heat purées. For helpful tips on freezing these purées for future use, see the Notes on Freezing Fruit, page 115.

No-heat purées

As the name suggests, these purées are made by blending fresh fruit directly, preserving the vibrant flavours that would otherwise diminish with the introduction of heat. Summer berries like strawberries, blackberries, raspberries and mulberries, as well as soft persimmons are best when undamaged by heat. A whisper of sugar added to fruit such as berries will help to release the natural juices when puréed. Start with 1 teaspoon of sugar for every 300g (10½oz) of fruit if the fruit is very ripe, increasing it by 2 teaspoons if the fruit seems firm.

For soft berries: Ensure the berries are clean and dry, removing any mouldy or bruised ones that may impact the final flavour. Place the fruit into the bowl of a food processor and scatter the sugar over the top. Blend until everything is nice and smooth. Alternatively, you can use a stick blender and a large bowl, but it is best to avoid a stand blender, as its strong, sharp blades may break

through the seeds, imparting a bitter flavour and sandy texture. Transfer the purée to a fine-mesh sieve nestled over a clean bowl and begin to press the purée through the sieve. I find the back of a ladle is the most effective way of extracting the purée, but a spoon or spatula will also work. Scrape the bottom of the sieve to pull away any precious purée clinging to it. The seeds can either be reserved or discarded. When making ice cream or semifreddo, I prefer adding smooth purée to the base, then stirring in some of the seeds for added texture.

For soft persimmons: Start with an astringent variety of persimmon (see page 179.) Check that the persimmons are ripe – they should be translucent and bursting through thin cracks in the flesh. Place a large-holed sieve over a bowl, remove the tops of the persimmons, and crush them into the sieve using clean hands. Then use the back of a ladle to push the remaining purée through the sieve, leaving only the skins to discard. Store it in a container with a piece of baking parchment placed on top to prevent further oxidation. The purée will keep in the refrigerator for 2–3 days or in the freezer for up to 3 months.

Flash-heat purées

In certain cases, a quick flash of hot heat is required to break down the fruit while preserving its fresh and vibrant flavour. This technique is particularly suitable for most stone fruits, as well as grapes, gooseberries, currants and rhubarb. For stone fruits, a quick burst of heat is necessary to penetrate the fruit and halt the enzymes that would otherwise lead to browning. When it comes to tougher fruits such as gooseberries, currants and rhubarb, a short cooking time helps soften the fibres and break down the fruit. Introducing a small amount of water to the pan serves a dual purpose: it prevents the fruit from burning from below, while creating steam that penetrates the fruit and speeds the cooking process. The precise amount of water needed will vary, with juicier fruits like peaches requiring less and fibrous fruits like currants and rhubarb demanding a bit more. Acid can also be added to preserve colour and enhance flavour, while a small amount of sugar will again help the fruit to break down. When adding the sugar, sprinkle a light spoonful over the fruit, avoiding the sides or bottom of the pan where it may easily burn. In all cases, you will want to cool the purée quickly to avoid overcooking. I transfer the cooked fruit directly into a clean bowl placed over another bowl filled with ice and stir to stop the cooking.

For stone fruits: While peaches should be blanched to remove their skins (refer to page 167), other stone fruits like apricots, cherries, nectarines, and plums can be cooked with the skins on. Slice the fruit in half and remove the stone. If the stones cling to the flesh, try to cut and remove as much of the flesh as possible. For apricots and plums, the stones can be cracked and kernels removed, then tied into a piece of muslin and placed into a pan with the fruit. (Alternatively, for cherries, peaches and nectarines, you may want to stir in a handful of peach leaves after cooking and just before chilling.) Place the fruit into a large saucepan or wide pot. If the fruit fills the pan more than halfway, then divide the fruit between two pans. Add a whisper of sugar, a squeeze of lemon juice, and just enough water to coat the bottom of the pan. Place over a high heat with a secure lid on top. Once the fruit begins to boil, use a whisk or potato masher to bash the fruit until it is fully submerged in its own liquids. Don't worry too much if the fruit is not completely broken down at this stage. When it reaches a second boil, remove it from

the heat. If using peach leaves, stir them into the purée at this point. Quickly and carefully transfer the purée to a bowl set over another bowl filled with ice and stir continuously until chilled. Pass the purée through a large sieve or food mill to separate the skins from the flesh. For a smoother purée, transfer it to a blender. Otherwise, store it in an airtight container with a piece of baking parchment placed on top to prevent further oxidation. This will keep in the refrigerator for 2–3 days.

For grapes, gooseberries and currants: Begin by rinsing the fruit under cool water, then pull the fruit away from the stems, and transfer to a saucepan or wide pot. If the pan is more than half full, divide the fruit between two pans. Add a whisper of sugar over the top of the fruit and just enough water to come 3–4cm (1½in) up the side of the pan. For grapes, consider adding a splash of red wine vinegar; for gooseberries add a squeeze of lemon or lime juice, then place over a high heat with a secure lid on top. When the fruit begins to boil, use a whisk or potato masher to crush the fruit until it is fully submerged in its own liquid. Check the side of the pan and if juices are beginning to sizzle or burn, reduce to a medium heat. Don't worry if the fruit isn't broken down at this stage. Once it comes to a second boil, check to see if the fruit has completely collapsed and if not, break it up with the whisk. Grapes and currants may require additional time to break down, so cook for another 3–4 minutes if needed. Quickly and carefully transfer the purée to a clean bowl placed upon another bowl filled with ice and stir to stop the cooking. Once the purée is room temperature, pass through a fine-mesh sieve using the back of a ladle, leaving only the skins and seeds behind. Scrape the bottom of the sieve to pull away the extra purée and store in the refrigerator for up to 4 days.

For rhubarb: Rhubarb tends to burn more easily, and therefore requires more monitoring. The day before you plan to cook the purée, rinse the stalks of rhubarb under cold water and remove the tops just under the leaves, as well as the tough bits near the ends. Chop the stalks into pieces the width of two fingers, and place them into a container. For every 250g (9oz) of rhubarb, add 1 teaspoon of sugar, and allow to macerate overnight. (If you are short on time, the rhubarb can be left for 2–3 hours in a warm corner of the kitchen. Use it once all the sugar dissolves and the rhubarb has begun to release its juices.) The next day, place the rhubarb into a pan along with all its liquid. If there is not enough liquid to coat 2–3cm (1in) up the sides of the pan, add a splash of water. At this point, I sometimes add a vanilla pod, or the zest and juice of a blood orange. Again, for every 250g (9oz) of rhubarb, add an additional 90g (3¼oz) of sugar. Cover and cook over a medium–high heat for 5–10 minutes until the rhubarb breaks down completely, stirring occasionally to prevent it from catching on the bottom. Transfer to a clean bowl placed over another bowl filled with ice and stir to stop the cooking. Once the purée is room temperature, you can blend it until it is silky and smooth. At this point, the rhubarb will keep in the refrigerator for up to 4 days.

Plain Ice-cream Base

MAKES 1 LITRE (34FL OZ)

400ml (14fl oz) double
 cream
400ml (14fl oz) milk
130g (4½oz) caster sugar
130g (4½oz) egg yolks
 (from 6–7 eggs)
1 tsp salt

Place the double cream, milk, sugar and salt into a heavy, non-reactive saucepan and place over a medium heat. Take two large bowls and add iced water in the largest bowl, nestling the other bowl inside. Sit a fine-mesh sieve over the top bowl and set it aside somewhere nearby.

Whisk the yolks in a separate bowl, then wrap a tea towel around the base to stabilize it. Once the milk mixture begins to simmer, gradually add the hot milk to the yolks, whisking constantly as you pour. (If your saucepan is too heavy to hold with one hand, then use a ladle or small cup.) Return the mixture to the pan and reduce to a medium–low heat. Gently cook, stirring constantly, until the mixture is thick enough to coat the back of a spoon. Remove from the heat and strain the mixture through the fine-mesh sieve into the cold bowl over ice. Once the ice cream base is properly chilled, pour into a container and store in the refrigerator overnight, or up to 3 days.

Jostaberry ice-cream

Jostaberries, in the simplest terms, are a cross between a gooseberry and blackcurrant, with a flavour that can be described just like that. This ice cream can also be made using blackcurrants, if jostaberries are hard to source.

SERVES 10–12

600g (1lb 5oz) jostaberries (stems removed before weighing)

100–200g (3½–7oz) caster sugar

500ml (18fl oz) Plain Ice Cream Base (see opposite page)

Place the jostaberries into a pan and add a whisper of sugar over the fruit, avoiding the sides of the pan where the sugar may burn, then pour in just enough water to come 3–4cm (1–1½in) up the side of the pan. Place over a high heat with a secure lid on top to seal in the steam. When the fruit begins to boil, remove the lid and lightly bash the fruit until it is fully submerged in its own liquid. It is fine if the fruit is not completely broken down at this stage. If the sides are beginning to sizzle or burn, reduce the heat slightly and cover once again. Once it comes to a second boil, check to see if the fruit is completely broken down. If the fruit needs more time, cook for another 3–4 minutes. When the fruit is broken down, quickly and carefully transfer the purée to a bowl set over another bowl filled with ice, and stir continuously until chilled. Pass through a fine-mesh sieve using the back of a ladle, leaving only the skins and seeds behind. Scrape the bottom of the sieve to pull away the precious purée clinging to it.

Measure 450g (1lb) of jostaberry purée and place it into a blender jug with the ice cream base and 100g (3½oz) of sugar, then blitz until smooth. Alternatively, you can use a stick blender in the bowl, or even a whisk. Taste the ice-cream base and add more sugar, or purée if desired. Churn the mixture in an ice-cream maker following the manufacturer's instructions.

Serving suggestions: Serve with cream and soft, pillowy Almond Meringues (page 116) or with Sugared Rose Petals (page 116).

Loganberry Semifreddo

There are few better ways to enjoy fruit than in a cold, creamy, intensely flavoured semifreddo – especially one made with sharp, inky berries. However tempting it may be, wait until the berries are in full swing before making this. You will be rewarded with the flavour of sweet sun-ripened berries, which will make all the difference.

SERVES 8

neutral oil (like grapeseed),
    for greasing
320ml (11fl oz) double
    cream, chilled
340g (11¾oz) loganberry
    purée (see Notes)
2 teaspoons lemon juice
3 egg yolks
110g (3¾oz) caster sugar
small pinch of salt

loganberry seeds (optional,
    see Note)

Measure two pieces of baking parchment, each approximately 40cm (16in) long. Take the first piece and fold the short ends into thirds like a letter. This will give you a long strip of baking parchment. Lightly oil a 450g (1lb) loaf tin and place the long strip of parchment across the middle of the tin. The ends will serve as handles when you need to release the semifreddo. Use the second piece of parchment to line the walls of the loaf tin, with plenty of overhang to cover the top of the semifreddo. Place the tin into the freezer.

Next, pour the cold cream into a large bowl. It may seem like a small amount of cream in such a large bowl, but you'll need the space to add the sabayon later. Whip the cream until the whisk begins to leave streaks, but stop before the cream forms soft peaks. Put the cream into the refrigerator to keep cold while you make your sabayon.

Bring a pan of water to the boil and place the loganberry purée, lemon juice, egg yolks, sugar and salt into the bowl of a stand mixer and place on top of the pan of boiling water. Check to make sure the bottom of the bowl is not in contact with the water. Whisk continuously until the mixture thickens slightly (reaching around 80°C/176°F). Observe how the sabayon changes – the bubbles will go from large to small and the whisk will leave trails as the mixture thickens and becomes glossy. Immediately remove from the heat and transfer to a stand mixer fitted with the whisk attachment. Whisk on medium–high speed until the sabayon reaches room temperature or the bowl no longer feels warm to the touch.

Take the cream out of the refrigerator and gently whisk until it holds soft peaks. Working quickly but carefully so as not to lose the volume you've created, fold one-third of the loganberry sabayon into the cream using the whisk. Switch to a spatula and fold in the rest of the sabayon along with the seeds if you are using them. Take the loaf tin from the freezer and pour the semifreddo into the tin. Cover with the overhanging parchment and place it back into the freezer for at least 5 hours or overnight.

For the loganberry purée, start with 450–500g (1lb–1lb 2oz) whole loganberries. Blitz using either a food processor or stick blender. Strain the purée through a sieve and keep the seeds. Once the semifreddo is mixed, you can fold in half of the loganberry seeds for extra texture if desired.

Twenty minutes before you are ready to serve, transfer the semifreddo to the refrigerator. Just before serving, get a tray or wide bowl and fill with warm water, then dip the tin into the warm water to help release the semifreddo. Use a tea towel to remove excess water from the bottom of the tin, then place the serving plate on the top of the tin. Carefully flip the semifreddo over, gently tugging on the overhanging parchment, until it falls onto the plate. If it won't release from the tin, flip it back over and either dip it into the warm water again, or run a knife over the edges of the semifreddo until it is loose.

Serving suggestions: Slice the semifreddo and serve with Peaches in Syrup (page 164) or a scattering of Sugared Rose Petals (page 116). Or scoop into a bowl with Mixed Berry Compote (page 109) and Soft Almond Cookies (page 141).

VARIATIONS
The creamy nature of this dessert works equally well with sharp, intense fruit like blackcurrant, gooseberries, rhubarb, plums, damsons or apricots.

Roasting Fruit

Roasting fruit is a fantastic way to intensify its flavour. The best fruits for roasting are those that can withstand high heat without losing their shape, and whose flavours will deepen rather than diminish. These include figs, cherries, apricots, plums, blueberries, pears and rhubarb. To prevent burning, add a small amount of liquid to the fruit, which could be in the form of juice, spirits or plain water. Extra aromatics like vanilla, citrus zest, spices or sturdy herbs may be added at the beginning. However, delicate herbs or other scented leaves should be added towards the end, allowing just enough time for their fragrance to mingle with the juices of the fruit.

To retain the shape of fruits like figs, apricots and plums, sugar is added midway through the cooking process. Sugar draws out the fruit's natural juices, but adding it too early can cause the fruit to collapse in the oven. By delaying the addition of sugar, the fruit's flavour has more time to concentrate under the heat. When sprinkling sugar on any fruit, whether using your fingers or a spoon, try to maintain a distance of about 20cm (8in) to allow the sugar to fall broadly and evenly over the top. This is also a great opportunity to get to know your oven if you don't already. Check the temperature with an oven thermometer to make sure it's calibrated correctly, and familiarize yourself with the hot spots and cool spots. These insights will guide your cooking and prevent burning mishaps.

When selecting a roasting vessel, a heavy ceramic dish is ideal for the high heat. Choose one that comfortably accommodates all the fruit you intend to roast. Don't worry if you don't have a special roasting dish; you can work with what you have in your cupboards, whether it's a pie dish, cazuela or casserole. A cast-iron pan or even a loaf tin will do. It's important to arrange the sliced fruit side by side in neat rows to ensure even cooking. If the fruit is overcrowded, it may steam instead of roast, but if it's too spread out, it could dry out and burn. If your roasting tray looks sparse, it's better to fill it with more fruit than you need for this reason. Extra roasted fruit can be saved and spooned over yoghurt for breakfast or served with cake or ice cream.

Roasted Apricots with Muscat de Beaumes de Venise

Ripe apricots and Muscat de Beaumes de Venise, at their best, share a beguiling scent of honey and sweet nectar. This makes them a perfect combination for this simple dish. If you have difficulty sourcing muscat dessert wine, particularly one that won't strain your budget, feel free to experiment with other white dessert wines such as Sauternes or Vin Santo.

SERVES 4–6

1kg (2lb 4oz) ripe, fragrant
  apricots
4 tablespoons Muscat de
  Beaumes de Venise
1 vanilla pod, split
  (optional)
2–4 tablespoons caster
  sugar

Preheat the oven 220°C/425°F/gas mark 7.

Halve the apricots and remove the stones, saving them for another purpose (refer to Noyau Extract, page 135). Arrange the apricot halves closely together in a ceramic dish. Sprinkle 2 tablespoons of Muscat de Beaumes de Venise over the apricots, and add just enough water to lightly coat the bottom of the dish (approximately 2–3 tablespoons). Place the dish in the preheated oven for 7 minutes.

Meanwhile, scrape the seeds from the vanilla pod then place the seeds in a bowl along with the sugar. Using your fingertips, rub the vanilla into the sugar and set it aside. Once the apricots are hot and gently sizzling around the edges, evenly distribute the sugar mixture over the top. Continue roasting for another 7–10 minutes, until the sugar has dissolved into the fruit and the edges have started to darken. The fruit should be tender while retaining its shape. Remove the dish from the oven and cut a small corner from one of the apricots to taste. Adjust the sweetness by adding the remaining sugar if desired. Sprinkle the remaining 2 tablespoons of Muscat de Beaumes de Venise over the apricots, and allow them to cool on a wire rack.

Sweet Roasted Cherries with Peach Leaves

Pitting cherries before cooking certainly makes them easier to eat, so the following recipes have been written that way. However, roasting cherries whole, with their little stones intact, imparts a delicate fragrance reminiscent of bitter almonds (so keep them whole if you like). And if you happen to have fresh peach leaves available, you can take this flavour to the next level by adding them to the cherries at the very end.

SERVES 4–6

400g (14oz) pitted cherries
½ vanilla pod, split
40g (1½oz) caster sugar
zest of ½ lemon
4 tablespoons kirsch,
    amaretto or water
5 peach leaves, clean and
    dry (optional)

Preheat the oven to 200°C/400°F/gas mark 6.

Place the sugar in a small bowl, then use a knife to scrape the vanilla seeds from the pod and add them to the sugar. Use your fingertips to rub the vanilla into the sugar, ensuring that the seeds are evenly dispersed. Next, put the cherrries, vanilla sugar, lemon zest and kirsch in a baking dish that comfortably accommodates the cherries in a single layer. Give the dish a little shake to coat the cherries, then slide into the hot oven. Roast for 10 minutes, then give the dish another little shake and rotate it 180 degrees. Continue roasting until the cherry skins begin to sizzle and wrinkle slightly. Open the oven and pull out the dish halfway. Working quickly, gently crush the peach leaves in one hand and scatter them over the cherries. With your other hand, carefully shake the hot dish a few times to incorporate the leaves, and return it to the oven for 1 minute. Remove the pan and let the cherries rest, shaking the pan occasionally to distribute the flavours. Serve warm or room temperature.

Serving suggestions: Serve with Little Chocolate Pots with Roasted Cherries and Kirsch Cream (page 145), Almond Cake (page 175) or Chocolate Tart (page 192).

Savoury Roasted Cherries with Thyme

Peppery and herbaceous flavours, such as olive oil and thyme, delicately balance the sweetness of cherries in this savoury dish.

SERVES 4–6

400g (14oz) pitted cherries
½ teaspoon salt
¼ teaspoon pepper
zest of ½ lemon
a few sprigs of thyme
2 tablespoons olive oil
4 teaspoons brandy or red
   wine (optional)

Preheat the oven to 200°C/400°F/gas mark 6.

Put the cherries, salt, pepper, lemon zest and thyme in a baking dish that comfortably accommodates the cherries in a single layer. Drizzle olive oil over the fruit and if desired, add a splash of brandy. Give the dish a gentle shuffle to ensure the cherries are coated, then immediately place it in the preheated oven. Roast for 10 minutes, then give the dish another little shake and rotate it 180 degrees. Continue roasting until the cherry skins begin to sizzle and wrinkle slightly. Remove the pan from the oven and allow the cherries to rest, shaking the pan occasionally to distribute the flavours.

Serving suggestions: Serve with Pan-fried Duck Breast (page 86) or Goat's Cheese Soufflés (page 147).

Roasted Figs on Fig Leaves

The oils of the fig leaf are incredibly aromatic and, when cooked with figs, have a way of underscoring the fruit's natural earthy flavour. Liquid added to the figs will keep the fruit moist from below, while the tips crisp, curl and caramelize under the heat. Watch as the liquid begins to bubble, taking in the flavour of the leaves below and reducing into a luscious velvety sauce. In this recipe I make a fig starter, which is essentially leftover figs cooked in water (see below). If you don't have enough figs to make a fig starter, simply splash a layer of marsala, sherry or water over the figs. You may not have enough liquid for a sauce, but the additional liquid should prevent the figs from drying out.

SERVES 6

4–6 fig leaves

2kg (4lb 8oz) fresh ripe figs

about 150ml (5½oz) (see opposite) or water

splash of dry marsala or sherry (optional)

2–4 tablespoons caster sugar

fresh thyme sprigs (for savoury figs)

Preheat the oven to 250°C/485°F or its highest setting. Rinse the fig leaves under cool water to remove any dirt, then pat them dry and place them into a ceramic dish, making sure that they cover the bottom of the dish: it is fine if they overlap slightly.

Next, slice the fresh ripe figs in half and arrange them in rows on top of the fig leaves so that they are touching side by side. Pour the fig starter in between the figs so that their bottoms are completely submerged, then add a splash of dry marsala or sherry over the fruit.

Roast the figs in the oven for 4–5 minutes until the juices begin to bubble and steam. Pull the dish out of the oven, and sprinkle the caster sugar over the top of the fruit. Start with the smaller amount for savoury figs, or the larger amount for sweet. If making savoury figs, add the fresh thyme now. Place the dish back into the oven and set a timer for 4 minutes. The figs are ready when the centres start to swell, and the edges darken and caramelize.

Remove the dish from the oven and carefully place onto a wire rack to rest. The figs will drink up the flavour of the liquid and any remaining liquid will thicken into a glossy sauce as it cools. To serve the figs, carefully pick them up by the tip and run through the sauce to coat.

Serving suggestions: Serve alongside Almond Cake (page 175) or over Honey Lavender Ice Cream (page 164).

FIG STARTER

A fruit starter, in this context, is any bit of fruit that is cooked in plenty of water, then strained. It could be the start to a sauce, glaze, jelly or roasting liquid. Not only can it be used to enhance the flavour of a dish, but it is a great way to use up damaged or overripe fruit. Whether you are picking figs off the tree or selecting them at your local market, look for the ripe soft figs, with a deep red centre.

Select ripe figs for roasting and set them aside, then allot the overripe figs to the starter. Using your hands, tear the figs open and place into a pan. Fill the pan with water until all the figs are comfortably submerged. Lightly bash the fruit and bring to the boil, then turn down the heat and simmer for 30 minutes. Strain through a fine-mesh sieve, and gently push down on the fruit with the back of a spoon or ladle. Once you have extracted as much liquid as possible, use immediately or transfer to a jar and store in the refrigerator for up to a week.

TECHNIQUES FOR COOKING WITH FRUIT

Poaching Fruit

Poaching is the art of gently cooking fruit in a light syrup, often scented with aromatics or wine. You will want to begin with fruit that is firm but ripe. Ripe fruit is necessary to get the most flavour, however fruit that is too soft could break down while cooking and should be reserved for another purpose, like purée (page 14). Loquats, apricots, cherries, peaches, nectarines, plums, greengages, pears, quinces and kumquats all lend themselves well to poaching. Aromatics should be in tune with the seasons and complement the fruit being poached. Citrus peel and zest, warm spices, wine (red, white or rosé), dessert wine, noyau (page 135), herbs or even tea are all delightful additions. When using citrus, peel the zest directly into the sugar syrup then squeeze in the juice. For whole spices like cinnamon, cardamom, clove, or black pepper, wrap them in a piece of muslin to prevent the bits of spices from embedding into the fruit as it softens. Dried fruits, such as figs, currants, prunes, sultanas and apricots, can also be poached to create a nice accompaniment for breakfast, cheese or roasted meats.

Select a sturdy saucepan or large pot with a heavy base. The fruit should occupy no more than two-thirds of the pot, leaving enough space for the poaching liquid to comfortably submerge the fruit. Avoid pushing the fruit to the bottom of the pan where it may burn, and make sure it does not protrude out of the top, which can result in uneven cooking.

Warm the water and sugar together until the sugar dissolves, then add your chosen aromatics. If you are working with fruits that oxidize easily, like peaches or pears, slip them into the syrup as you prepare them. Cover with a piece of baking parchment and poke a few holes to allow the steam to escape. If the fruit seems to be peeking out of the liquid, either add more syrup or place a smaller lid on top of the parchment to gently weigh the fruit down. To remove the lid later, use a pair of tongs and a tea towel to carefully lift the lid, making sure any hot liquid falls back into the pan. Place the pot over a medium–high heat and bring it to a boil, then reduce the heat to a very gentle, champagne simmer (page 28) and continue to cook until barely done. Most fruit is ready when a knife effortlessly pierces through it. Pears and quinces will have a translucent core and require longer poaching times, while ripe stone fruits benefit from shorter cooking. Poaching times can vary significantly for each fruit, so begin checking pears after 40 minutes and stone fruits after 10 minutes. Quinces may take several hours, while most dried fruit can simmer for 10–15 minutes and then be left off the heat for 30 minutes or preferably overnight.

Poached fruit can be enjoyed on its own, accompanied by a jug of cream or a dollop of crème fraîche. Alternatively, serve it over ice cream or alongside slices of freshly baked cake. Arrange fanned poached pears next to the ginger cake (page 90) or tuck slices of poached quince between layers of fresh apples before baking a tart (page 218). You may also consider serving poached fruit alongside another fresh fruit. Simply sweeten the fresh fruit by tossing it briefly in the poaching liquid.

Some of my favourite poached and fresh fruit combinations are opposite.

POACHED	FRESH
Vanilla-poached peaches	*Raspberries*
Wine-poached pears (page 30)	*Blackberries*
Honey-poached quinces	*Pomegranates*
Poached kumquats (page 65)	*Strawberries*
Tea-poached prunes	*Blood oranges*

Poaching Fruit

Poached Quinces

When selecting quinces, I search for firm, yellow ones and lift them to my nose – if they are fragrant, they're likely to be good candidates for poaching.

SERVES 10

1 vanilla pod, split and
  seeds removed
225g (8oz) caster sugar
1 litre (1¾ pints) water
1 organic orange
4–5 quinces

NOTE:

Keeping the core intact during poaching has several benefits; for one, the cores are a lot easier to remove once the flesh of the quinces has softened. Furthermore, the core and seeds are rich in pectin, which cooks into the poaching liquid, and adds both body and texture.

Start by gently rubbing the vanilla seeds with the sugar, releasing the aromatic seeds, then pour it into a large pan and add the water. Peel the zest from the orange directly into the pan, then squeeze in the juice and add the rest of the orange. Place over a medium–high heat to dissolve the sugar, then remove from the heat and let it cool.

Peel the quinces and quarter them from stem to base, leaving the cores intact. As you peel and prepare the quince quarters, slip each one into the liquid. Once they're all done, cover the pan with a round piece of baking parchment and place a smaller lid directly on top of the parchment to keep the quinces fully submerged. Bring the liquid to a gentle boil, then reduce the heat to a champagne simmer (see below).

The cooking time will vary depending on the ripeness of the quinces. They're done once they turn a deep amber and are soft but still hold their shape – verify this by piercing the flesh with the tip of a sharp knife. It's not uncommon for the process to take 4 hours or even longer. If the quinces are soft but pale in colour, turn the heat to the lowest setting and let them sit for an additional 2–3 hours. Remove from the heat and cool to room temperature (or overnight). Use a wide spoon to transfer the quinces to a container, then strain the liquid over them. Store in the refrigerator for up to 14 days.

THE CHAMPAGNE SIMMER

A gentle boil is often required during poaching to retain the shape of the fruit and prevent overcooking. When describing this technique to new chefs I often tell them to look for a 'champagne simmer', i.e when the bubbles lifting from the bottom of the pan resemble the tiny bubbles in a glass of freshly opened champagne. Too much heat can lead to uneven cooking or increase the chances of overcooked fruit; too little heat will not cook the fruit at all. A champagne simmer allows the syrup to gently penetrate the fruit while leaving it intact. This technique is also used for candying citrus peel (page 54), to keep the peel soft and prevent it from hardening or burning.

ELEVATING FLAVOUR WITH ACIDITY AND SPIRITS

It is often tempting to reach for a slice of lemon whenever your fruit dish needs a bit of brightness. Yet different fruits have a diverse array of flavours and each one will respond to different types of acidity. Strawberries and peaches love lemon, while rhubarb and quinces respond favourably to the more subtle acidity of oranges. Mangoes come alive with a squeeze of lime juice, while the velvety fig prefers a lift from raspberry or marsala. Consider adding wine to grapes or even offer them a splash of red wine vinegar. For blueberries, cherries and even apples, reach for the lemon once more.

The same principle applies to wines and spirits. Prunes in Armagnac make for a classic and reliable combination. Muscat de Beaumes de Venise seems to complement just about everything. Match *eaux des vie* with their respective fruits: Calvados with apples, Poire Williams with pears, and kirsch with cherries. Homemade noyau liqueur (page 135) would amplify anything made with apricot, and a small dash added to stone fruits would round out the aromatic almond notes naturally present. Partner marsala with figs or caramelized pears and let sherry accompany raspberries or quinces. Venture into more herbaceous spirits by cooking pastis with figs, bitters with grapefruit, Chartreuse with pears or vermouth with blood oranges.

Wine-Poached Pears

The instructions for poaching pears are the same for any of the recipes below. The best varieties of pears for poaching will be firm when ripe, and include Bosc, Conference or Anjou. However, feel free to use any variety that is available to you. Before you begin, check all of your fruit for ripeness. The pears should smell fragrant and give slightly when pressed near the base. The flesh should yield easily under a sharp peeler, but if it sounds like wood scraping against sandpaper, or the flesh looks dry instead of juicy, your pears will need more time to ripen. The poaching process may seem lengthy but the end result is well worth it. Once well chilled, the poached pears can be stored for up to 2 weeks and used in a variety of dishes, some of which I have mentioned opposite.

SERVES 8–10

RED WINE POACHING LIQUID

750ml (26fl oz) fruity red
wine
250ml (9fl oz) water
180g (6oz) caster sugar
zest of 1 orange
1 cinnamon stick (or cassia
 bark)
2 cloves
1 star anise
3 black peppercorns
pinch of salt
4–5 medium pears (about 625g/1lb
 6oz)

Other fruits
Cherries
Quinces

WHITE WINE POACHING LIQUID

750ml (26fl oz) fruity white wine
250ml (9fl oz) water
180g (6oz) caster sugar
1 vanilla pod, scraped and stirred into
 the sugar
zest and juice of 1 lemon
pinch of salt
4–5 medium pears (about 625g/1lb
 6oz)

Other fruits
Peaches
Nectarines
Plums

VIN SANTO AND HONEY

375ml (13fl oz) Vin Santo
200ml (7fl oz) water
50g (1¾oz) caster sugar
50g (1¾oz) honey
zest and juice of ½ lemon
pinch of salt
3–4 medium pears (about 450g/1lb
 6oz)

Other fruits
Loquats
Greengages

Techniques for Cooking with Fruit

Place all your chosen poaching liquid ingredients into a heavy-based pan large enough to fit 4–5 pears. If using spices, tie them into a piece of muslin before adding to the pan. Place over a medium heat and bring to a simmer. Stir to dissolve the sugar, then remove from the heat and allow to cool slightly.

Peel each pear from the top to the base, taking care to remove as little fruit as possible. After you peel each pear, slip it directly into the poaching liquid to prevent it from browning. Once all the pears are submerged into the pot, cover with a piece of baking parchment and heat to a gentle boil. Watch the pears during this early stage, the moment the liquid begins to bubble, reduce the heat to a very gentle, champagne simmer (page 28). Cook for about 40 minutes until the pears are poached all the way through, but still hold their shape. To check it is done, slice a pear in half from top to bottom. If the centre looks raw and opaque or begins to brown after a minute or so, it is underdone and needs more time. Once the pears are cooked, remove from the heat and, using a wide slotted spoon, carefully transfer them to a container. Pour the poaching liquid over the top and allow to cool to room temperature. Cover the pears and store in the refrigerator.

Serving suggestions: Red wine-poached pears with Almond Cake (page 175) and crème fraîche, white wine-poached pears with Ginger Cake (page 90) and blackberries, Vin Santo poached pears with Frozen Yoghurt-Honey Parfait (page 123).

Techniques for Cooking with Fruit

A CASE FOR SERVING FRESH FRUIT

A beautiful bowl of fruit can elevate any meal. It can punctuate the end of a delicious dinner or simply extend the time spent gathered around the table. It can complement a cheese plate, bridging the gap between the main dish and dessert, and allowing time to savour the last sips of wine. I often end dinner with a bowl of fruit selected for its ripeness and taste, possibly paired with cheese, biscuits or both. It seems to prolong the magic of a special dinner with family or friends.

The simplicity of a fruit bowl demands thought and consideration. Select a wide bowl or platter to avoid overcrowding. Ensure the fruit is fresh and at room temperature, with the exception of cherries (see A Case for Cold Cherries, page 142). Always taste the fruit first to avoid disappointment at the table. Add a dash of alcohol (page 29), or adorn the bowl with matching leaves or edible flowers, ensuring they don't wilt. Scatter fresh rose petals just before serving or even add Sugared Rose Petals (page 116), or a few Honeyed Walnuts (page 201). Add the leaves of grape, fig, lemon or cherry. In autumn, persimmon or chestnut leaves bring amber hues. During winter, accent fragrant citrus with dates, prunes, fresh walnuts or hazelnuts.

SEASONAL FRUIT BOWLS

SPRING	*Late-season tangerines and dates with lemon leaves • First-of-the-season strawberries with kumquats • Apricots • Chilled cherries with cherry leaves • Loquats with a splash of Vin Santo*
SUMMER	*Strawberries and candied mint leaves (use method on page 116) • Cherries, raspberries and blueberries • Peaches and golden raspberries • Nectarines, raspberries and rose petals • Plums and blackberries on plum leaves*
AUTUMN	*Chardonnay grapes on grape leaves • Pears and steamed chestnuts • Figs and autumn raspberries on fig leaves • Mulberries on a plate • Firm persimmons on persimmon leaves • Soft and translucent persimmons in a bowl with a spoon • New season apples with blackberries and fresh (wet) walnuts*
WINTER	*Tangerines and plump prunes on tangerine leaves • Mandarins and dates • Candied citrus peel and lightly roasted almonds • Slices of pink Navel oranges with a splash of red vermouth*

CITRUS

LEMON, ORANGE, CLEMENTINE, GRAPEFRUIT, LIME, KUMQUAT

Bright globes of citrus, with their clean, zesty flavour, bring a joyful touch to numerous winter dishes. The refreshing juice of clementines and oranges provides the ideal foundation for a winter salad or a light sorbet, while the aromatic oils from the zest of lime or bergamot can be used to perfume broths and sauces. This wide range of flavours makes citrus incredibly versatile. Fresh clementine juice complements orange blossom, bay leaf or prosecco. Combine fresh oranges and grapefruit with raw fennel for a refreshing salad or pair them with a delicate, flaky fish. The subtle bitterness of kumquats harmonizes with chocolate or espresso, and when made into marmalade, Seville oranges sit happily alongside the flavours of brandy or rye.

As for lemons, the best ones found in Europe come from the sun-drenched groves of Amalfi and Sicily. Their juice is punchy and their skins are aromatic. At the peak of lemon season, it's enough to rub your fingers along the skin of the fruit to release the shiny fragrant oils. For me, growing up on the west coast of America, the golden glow of Meyer lemons could be seen weighing down the branches that spilled over backyard fences. Originally from China, today Meyer lemons are found across the US, as well as in Australia and Europe. This coveted variety is prized for its mellower acidity, creamy pith and floral zest.

LEMON PAIRINGS

NUTS AND SEEDS	*Almond, macadamia, peanut, pecan, pistachio, pine nut*
FLOWERS, LEAVES AND HERBS	*Elderflower, lavender, orange blossom, rose, bay leaf, lemongrass, mint, rosemary, chervil, chive, dill, thyme*
SPICES	*Black pepper, caraway, cardamon, fennel, ginger, nutmeg*
FRUITS	*Apple, blueberry, cherry, coconut, gooseberry, nectarine, other citrus, peach, raspberry, strawberry*
VEGETABLES	*Asparagus, caper, celery, chicory, fennel, lettuce, olive, summer squash*
FLOURS	*Barley, buckwheat, khorasan, oat, polenta, rice, semolina, spelt, whole wheat*
WINES AND SPIRITS	*Rosé, Sauternes, sparkling wine, vermouth, white wine, brandy, gin, kirsch, vodka*
DAIRY, MEAT AND FISH	*Brown butter, buttermilk, fresh ricotta, goat's curd, mascarpone, yoghurt, chicken, fish, oyster, shellfish*
OTHER FLAVOURS	*Caramel, honey, mustard*

CLASSIC COMBINATIONS WITH LEMON

ALMOND • CARAWAY | GOOSEBERRY • GINGER | RASPBERRY • KIRSCH | SEMOLINA • RICOTTA
PORK • MILK | ROSEMARY • OLIVE | STRAWBERRY • ELDERFLOWER
APPLE • CRÈME FRAÎCHE | MACADAMIA • ROSE | CHICKEN • CAPER

Lemon Ice Cream

The richness of sweet cream and the bright acidity of lemon are brought into balance in this ice cream. I like to use the aromatic lemons from Sicily with their shimmering skins that release a mist of oil when peeled. If pressed to choose, this ice cream would rank among my all-time favourite desserts.

SERVES 8–10

300ml (10fl oz) whole milk

300ml (10fl oz) double cream

320g (11½oz) caster sugar

4–5 lemons, plus extra for juice if needed

5 egg yolks

Place the milk, cream and sugar into a heavy-based saucepan. Peel strips from the lemon rind using a vegetable peeler and scrape away the white pith that would otherwise add bitterness to your ice cream. Store the zested lemons in the refrigerator until the following day. Add the zest to the saucepan and bring to the boil. Remove from the heat and allow the mixture to infuse for 30 minutes.

Before you start to make your ice cream, take two large bowls and place iced water in the largest bowl, nestling the other bowl inside. Sit a fine-mesh sieve over the top bowl and set it aside somewhere nearby. Whisk the yolks in a separate bowl, then wrap a tea towel around the base to stabilize it. Heat the milk and cream mixture and once it begins to simmer gradually add the hot milk to the yolks, whisking constantly as you pour. (If your saucepan is too heavy to hold with one hand, then use a ladle or small cup.) Return the mixture to the pan and reduce to a medium–low heat. Gently cook, stirring constantly until the mixture is thick enough to coat the back of a spoon. Remove from the heat and strain the mixture through the fine-mesh sieve into the cold bowl over ice. Continue to stir until the custard is completely chilled, then transfer to a container and store in the refrigerator overnight.

The next day, juice the lemons and strain out the pips. Measure out 330ml (11fl oz), reserving the extra lemon juice and setting both aside. Stir the measured lemon juice into the chilled ice cream base. Taste and adjust with more sugar or lemon juice if necessary. Churn in an ice-cream maker following the manufacturer's instructions, then place into the freezer until you are ready to serve.

VARIATION
Lemon Elderflower Ice Cream: Reduce the zest to 2 lemons. When the milk mixture comes to the boil, add 2 heads of elderflower and infuse for 2 minutes. Remove the elderflower and continue with the recipe as above. Once the custard has cooled, taste and, if the flavour of elderflower is faint, then add another head of elderflower to the cooled base and allow to infuse overnight. Remove the following day and add 250ml (9fl oz) lemon juice before churning.

Lemon Curd Tart

I first learned how to make this lemon curd at Chez Panisse and I have yet to find a recipe that rivals it. It has everything you want in a curd – silky texture, bold lemon flavour and a perfectly balanced sweetness. The following recipe is for a lemon tart. My head pastry chef at the time, Mary Jo, taught me to pour the hot curd directly into the pre-baked tart shell, resulting in a smooth and even set. I understand the recipe calls for a generous amount of eggs and yolks, but don't be put off. And rather than discarding the gorgeous egg whites, make a lemon meringue pie (page 40), or save them for a batch of soft pillowy meringues (page 116). (Egg whites also store well in the freezer for up to a year.) Someone once asked me 'Why add milk?' Caught off guard, I responded with the first thing that came to mind: 'It's like adding water to whisky, it helps to open the flavours.' Nearly a decade later I stand by that comment and the inclusion of milk in the recipe.

This recipe will yield enough curd for the tart, plus a little extra, which can be stored in glass jars for up to a week.

SERVES 10-12

25cm (10in) tart tin, lined with shortcrust pastry and blind baked (page 133)
400ml (14fl oz) lemon juice
zest of 7 lemons
340g (11¾oz) caster sugar
245g (9oz) unsalted butter
360g (12½oz) eggs (about 8 eggs)
230g (8oz) egg yolks (about 12 eggs)
1 tablespoon full-fat milk

First make the pastry case and bake following the recipe on page 133. Leave the oven on.

In a heavy-based saucepan, combine the lemon juice and zest, sugar and butter. In a separate bowl, whisk together the eggs, yolks and milk. Place the saucepan over medium heat, then wrap a tea towel around the base of the bowl to stabilize it, keeping it within reach. Give the lemon juice mixture a gentle stir to dissolve the sugar and melt the butter.

When the lemon mixture begins to simmer, slowly ladle it into the eggs in a steady stream, whisking as you go and taking care not to curdle the eggs. Return the mixture to the pan and, using a spatula, slowly and continuously stir until the curd coats the back of the spatula. You can use a whisk if the mixture seems lumpy but use it sparingly so as not to incorporate too much air.

Immediately strain through a sieve into the prepared tart tin and place it into the oven for 3 minutes. The tart is done when the edges are set but the centre has a gentle wobble. If the centre still seems loose, cook for another 2–3 minutes. Remove from the oven and allow it to cool completely before slicing.

Variations overleaf

CURD VARIATIONS

Lemon and Bergamot Curd: Reduce the lemon juice to 350ml (12fl oz) and add 50ml (1¾fl oz) bergamot juice. Use the zest of 6 lemons and add the zest of 1 bergamot. Increase the milk by ½ tablespoon and proceed with the recipe as above.

Yuzu Curd: Use the zest of 2 lemons and add the zest of 3 yuzus.

Passion Fruit Curd: Using fresh passion fruit (about 20–25), scoop and strain the pulp through a fine-mesh sieve, and reserve the seeds. Use 350ml (12fl oz) of passion fruit juice and add 50ml (1¾fl oz) of lime juice. Proceed with the recipe as above. At the very end, stir in half of the reserved passion fruit seeds, if you so desire.

LEMON MERINGUE PIE

Using the Lemon Curd Tart as its base, this Lemon Meringue Pie is a contemporary version of the classic dessert found in diners across America.

SERVES 10–12

Lemon Curd Tart (page 39)
120g (4¼oz) egg whites (about 3 eggs)
180g (6oz) caster sugar
¼ teaspoon cream of tartar
vanilla extract (optional)

Combine the egg whites and sugar in the bowl of a stand mixer and place over a bain-marie. Check to make sure the bottom of the bowl is not in contact with the water, then heat the mixture to 80°C (176°F), stirring constantly. Immediately transfer to a stand mixer fitted with the whisk attachment and mix on medium–high speed until cool. You can also use a hand-held electric whisk. Spread the pillowy meringue over the top of the cooled lemon curd tart and use a kitchen blowtorch to toast the meringue until it is beautifully browned and caramelized.

Lemon Confit Two Ways

Confit refers to food submerged in liquid or fat and cooked slowly over a long period of time. It was traditionally a method of preservation for meat, but vegetables like tomatoes and garlic may also be confited in oil. In the following recipes are two ways to confit lemons. One is savoury and the other is sweet, but the method is similar and both will preserve the lemons for several weeks, if not longer.

LEMON CONFIT IN OLIVE OIL

MAKES 500ML (18FL OZ)

300ml (10fl oz) olive oil,
  plus extra if necessary
1 teaspoon salt
3–4 black peppercorns
1 sprig of fresh rosemary
1 bay leaf
1 small shallot, thinly sliced
1 garlic clove, sliced
3 unwaxed lemons,
  preferably Meyer

Preheat the oven to 120°C/250°F/gas mark ½. Combine the first seven ingredients in a saucepan and heat until the oil is warm and shimmers slightly but before the ingredients begin to sizzle. Using a sharp knife and a stable hand, slice the lemons into thin pinwheels. If you encounter a pip, remove it with the tip of the knife. Arrange the lemon slices in a baking dish, slightly overlapping them like rooftop tiles. Carefully ladle the warm oil mixture over the lemons until they are fully submerged, topping up with extra oil if required. Cover with baking parchment, and bake for 1½–2 hours until the lemons are translucent throughout. Remove from the oven and carefully transfer them to a sterilized jar, where they will keep for up to a month.

Serve with Lemony Chicken Piccata (page 47), Sea Bass in Fish Broth (page 62), Slow-cooked Salmon (page 81) or chopped and stirred into Simple Vinaigrette (page 148).

LEMON CONFIT IN SUGAR SYRUP

MAKES 500ML (18FL OZ)

200g (7oz) caster sugar
200ml (7fl oz) water
¼ teaspoon salt
3 unwaxed lemons,
  preferably Meyer

Preheat the oven to 140°C/275°F/gas mark 1. Place the sugar, water and salt in a saucepan and heat until the sugar is dissolved, then remove from the heat. Slice and lay the lemons in a baking dish as above. Carefully pour the sugar syrup over the lemons so they are submerged, then cover with a piece of baking parchment. Bake for about 1½–2 hours until the lemons are translucent throughout. Remove from the oven and leave to cool, covered in the syrup. Once cool, they can be transferred to a sterilized jar with their syrup, and stored in the refrigerator for up to a month.

NOTE:
Substitute blood oranges for lemons for a striking decoration.

Serve over the Lemon Curd Tart (page 39) or use to decorate the Lemon Drizzle (page 43).

Lemon Drizzle

It's worth having a recipe for a classic lemon drizzle in your baking repertoire. I adore this particular version because it's reliable, full of lemon flavour, and the addition of buttermilk provides a tender crumb.

SERVES 8–10

For the cake
200g (7oz) flour
1¼ teaspoons baking powder
¼ teaspoon bicarbonate of soda
zest of 1 lemon
225g (8oz) caster sugar
135g (4¾oz) butter, room temperature
140g (5oz) eggs (2–3 eggs)
¼ teaspoon salt
175ml (6oz) buttermilk

For the lemon soak
2 tablespoons lemon juice, strained
1 tablespoon caster sugar

For the lemon icing
150g (5½oz) icing sugar, sifted
1–1½ tablespoons lemon juice, strained

Position a rack in the middle of the oven and preheat it to 160°C/325°F/gas mark 3. Grease a loaf tin with butter and lightly dust it with flour. Tap out any excess flour and line the bottom with baking parchment. Sift the flour, baking powder and bicarbonate of soda into a bowl. Set aside. Zest the lemon directly over the measured sugar then rub it together using the tips of your fingers. In a separate mixing bowl, beat the butter until smooth and satiny. Add the lemony sugar and continue to cream until the mixture becomes light in colour and fluffy in appearance.

Beat the eggs together and add to the butter and sugar, a third at a time, mixing until fully incorporated before adding the next third. Continue to cream the mixture, scraping the sides of the bowl once or twice. Once all the eggs have been added, the texture will be fluffy, light and increased in volume (it should resemble whipped cream cheese and the graininess should disappear). If you are using a stand mixture, remove the bowl now and proceed to mix by hand.

Gently fold in one-third of the dry ingredients, followed by half of the buttermilk. Repeat this process, alternating between the dry and wet ingredients. After each addition, scrape the sides of the bowl and continue mixing until the batter is smooth.

Pour the batter into the prepared loaf tin, smoothing out the top, and bake for 25–30 minutes. Rotate the cake and bake for another 15–20 minutes until a skewer inserted into the middle of the cake comes out clean.

While the cake is baking, make the lemon soak by combining the lemon juice and sugar together until the sugar dissolves. When the cake is done, transfer it to a wire rack (still in the tin) and use a skewer or toothpick to poke holes in the surface. Spoon the lemon soak over the top and allow it to cool in the tin. When you're ready to ice the cake, remove it from the tin by running a palette knife or butter knife along the edges. Turn out the cake and remove the parchment from the bottom. Place it back onto the rack while you prepare the icing. Put the sifted icing sugar into a bowl and add the smaller amount of lemon juice. Mix with a small spoon or spatula until all the icing sugar is dissolved. If the icing seems thick, you can thin it out with a bit more juice. Spoon the icing over the cake, covering the top completely and allowing any excess icing to drizzle down the sides. Leave the icing to set before serving.

Lemon and Buttermilk Dressing

This creamy, lemon-scented dressing is best reserved for sturdier lettuces like Romaine or Reine des Glaces. Autumn and winter chicories will also hold under the weight of this dressing and are great candidates in wintertime. If you would like to add more delicate leaves, toss them into the salad at the final moment before serving.

MAKES 350ML (12FL OZ)

125ml (4fl oz) buttermilk
200ml (7fl oz) Homemade
 Mayonnaise (see below)
zest of 2 lemons, plus juice
 of 1, strained
a handful of soft herbs,
 finely chopped (see
 Variations)
salt and black pepper

In a bowl, whisk together the buttermilk and mayonnaise. Stir in the remaining ingredients, then taste and adjust the flavours to your preference. Use immediately or store the dressing in a jar in the refrigerator for up to 3 days.

VARIATIONS
The choice of herbs for the dressing can be tailored to the time of year and the accompanying dish. For a chicken salad, consider using tarragon, parsley and summer savory. In the summertime, dress your lettuce with a blend of basil, mint and chives, scattering a few whole herbs throughout the salad. During winter, opt for parsley, chervil and chives and add a spoonful of mustard.

HOMEMADE MAYONNAISE

MAKES ABOUT 450ML (16FL OZ)

2 egg yolks
pinch of salt
1 teaspoon lemon juice or
 white wine vinegar
350ml (12fl oz) olive oil
1 teaspoon mustard
 (optional)

In a bowl, whisk together the egg yolks, salt and lemon juice. Place a tea towel under the bowl for stability, then whisk constantly while adding a scant teaspoon of oil. Continue whisking until the oil is completely absorbed before adding the next teaspoon. After you've added about half the oil, you may add the rest in a slow and steady stream. Taste and add more lemon juice or salt if needed. Homemade mayonnaise will keep if well-sealed in the refrigerator for up to 5 days.

VARIATION
To make aioli, crush one clove of garlic and add it to the yolk along with the salt and lemon juice. Proceed with the recipe above.

Lemon and Buttermilk Dressing

Lemony Chicken Piccata

Lemon, chicken and capers appear harmoniously together in a number of dishes, however my favourite version is in this Italian-American classic. Serve it with orzo, or buttermilk mashed potatoes and garlicky green beans.

SERVES 4

4 skinless chicken breasts
salt and pepper
140g (5oz) butter, separated
50ml (1¾ fl oz) oil
250g (8¼oz) flour
1 garlic clove, chopped
100ml (3½fl oz) white wine
100ml (3½fl oz) chicken stock
zest of 1 lemon, plus lemon wedges to serve
1 tablespoon lemon juice
2 tablespoons capers
handful of parsley

Begin by cutting each chicken breast in half, slicing through horizontally to create two thinner pieces. Place the slices between two pieces of baking parchment and gently pound until they're about 1.5cm (½in) thick. Season the chicken with salt, cover lightly and set aside for 30 minutes–1 hour.

When you're ready to cook, heat a large heavy-based frying pan over a medium-high heat then add 40g (1½oz) of the butter and the oil. Put the flour into a shallow bowl, then dredge each chicken cutlet in the flour, shaking off the excess. When the pan is hot and the butter begins to sizzle, place the cutlets into the hot pan, ensuring you don't overcrowd the pan (you may need to do this in two batches.) Allow the cutlets to cook for 3–5 minutes, waiting patiently before flipping them. Once they are crisp and golden-brown, and release easily from the bottom of the pan, flip them and quickly sear the other side for about 30 seconds. Transfer to a plate and set aside. Repeat with the remaining pieces of chicken.

Add the chopped garlic to the pan and let it sizzle briefly, but before it browns, add the white wine. Bring the liquid to the boil and let it reduce until it is nearly evaporated. Add the chicken stock and using a spatula, scrape and lift any browned bits from the bottom of the skillet. Add the lemon zest, juice, capers and the remaining butter, swirling them around to form a glossy emulsion. Place the chicken cutlets back into the pan, spooning the sauce over each piece until they are warmed through. Take the pan off the heat and let everything rest for 5 minutes.

Just before serving, garnish the dish with freshly chopped parsley and wedges of lemon.

CITRUS PAIRINGS

NUTS AND SEEDS	*Almond, chestnut, hazelnut, macadamia, pecan, pine nut, pistachio, walnut*
FLOWERS, LEAVES AND HERBS	*Elderflower, orange blossom, bay leaf, lemongrass, coriander, mint, parsley, rosemary*
SPICES	*Allspice, aniseed, cardamom, chilli, ginger, cinnamon, licorice, nutmeg*
FRUITS	*Currant, date, dried apricot, persimmon, pomegranate, prune, quince, rhubarb*
VEGETABLES	*Beetroot, carrot, chicory, endive, fennel, olive, parsnip, rocket, sweet potato, winter squash*
FLOURS	*Barley, buckwheat, khorasan, oat, polenta, rye, spelt*
WINES AND SPIRITS	*Champagne, white wine, bitters, bourbon, brandy, spiced rum, tequila, whisky*
DAIRY, MEAT AND FISH	*Buttermilk, fresh ricotta, goat's curd, mascarpone, yoghurt, chicken, duck, lamb, pork, quail, fish, shellfish*
OTHER FLAVOURS	*Brown sugar, black tea, caramel, chocolate, coffee, honey*

FAVOURITE COMBINATIONS WITH CITRUS

BLOOD ORANGE • PINE NUT • ROSEMARY | BLOOD ORANGE • COCONUT • SPICED RUM
BLOOD ORANGE • FENNEL • CRAB | BLOOD ORANGE • BEETROOT • PISTACHIO
CLEMENTINE • OLIVE • PARSLEY | CLEMENTINE • BAY LEAF
GRAPEFRUIT • BITTERS • YOGHURT | KUMQUAT • HAZELNUT • RICOTTA
KUMQUAT • CHOCOLATE • ESPRESSO COFFEE | LIME • SEA BASS • CORIANDER | MANDARIN • GINGER
ORANGE • ALMOND • ANISEED | SEVILLE ORANGE • BOURBON • RYE

Clementine Sorbet

The ideal citrus sorbet will have all the vibrancy and flavour of a glass of freshly pressed juice. There is no need for additional water or syrups here, this sorbet is just fruit and sugar. In my days as head pastry chef, I used to juice the clementines at 11am to churn into sorbet for lunch service at noon. If possible you may want to consider a similar timetable, allowing for extra time in the freezer if your sorbet is soft. To avoid disappointment, I would suggest tasting the clementines for flavour before you proceed.

SERVES 8–10

1 litre (1¾ pints) freshly squeezed clementine juice, from about 1.6–1.8kg (3½–4lb) of clementines
160–200g (5¾–7oz) caster sugar
squeeze of lemon juice

NOTE:
This sorbet is best served within a few hours of making but will keep up to a day or two before getting icy. If the sorbet is too hard to scoop, then soften in the refrigerator for 20 minutes before serving.

Juice the clementines when you are ready to spin your sorbet. Slice the citrus across the equator, then extract the juice, using a juicer or press. Whichever method you use, try not to apply too much pressure, or the bitterness of the pith will leach into the juice. Strain to remove the pulp and seeds, then remeasure.

When you have 1 litre (1¾ pints) of strained clementine juice, add 160g (5¾oz) sugar, then stir until it is completely dissolved. Taste and, if necessary, add more sugar for sweetness, or boost the acidity with a squeeze of lemon juice. Churn immediately in an ice-cream maker following the manufacturer's instructions, then place into the freezer until you are ready to serve.

Fresh Citrus Two Ways

BLOOD ORANGES IN CARAMEL

In this recipe caramel is enhanced by the zest and juice of the blood oranges. While the caramel is still warm, it is poured over pinwheels of citrus. The heat from the caramel is just enough to bring the fruit's raw acidity into balance, while maintaining its fresh flavour.

SERVES 4–6

4 blood oranges
300g (10½oz) caster sugar
¼ teaspoon cream of
   tartar (optional)
100ml (3½fl oz) water

Zest one of the blood oranges into a bowl. Juice the same orange, then strain the pulp and measure 50ml (1¾fl oz) of juice. Add this to the zest and reserve the rest of the juice for another purpose. Supreme the remaining oranges (page 59) and slice into pinwheels about 5mm (¼in) thick, then transfer to a wide heatproof bowl or baking tin.

Place the sugar into a heavy-based saucepan and add the cream of tartar (if using) and 25ml (1fl oz) of the water. Stir until the sugar is the consistency of wet sand, then cover with a lid and place over a high heat. Cook until the pan begins to steam, then remove the lid and continue to cook, undisturbed, until the sugar begins to colour slightly. Gently swirl the pan, then reduce the heat and continue to cook to a rich amber caramel. Caramel will often appear darker in the pan, so to check the true colour of the caramel, place a couple of droplets on a white, heatproof plate. Once the droplets are the colour you are looking for, remove the pan from the heat and stir in the remaining 75ml (2½fl oz) water, then transfer to a heatproof container and add the orange juice and zest. Leave the zest to infuse for 10 minutes, then strain the warm caramel over the oranges and cool to room temperature.

Citrus in a Lightly Sweetened Citrus Juice

This is a great way to prepare citrus for a light sorbet, or the Ginger Cake (page 90). Feel free to use a mix of fruit here. The bowl looks quite impressive with a dazzling array of citrus. I often make this for breakfast to spoon over a bowl of thick yoghurt with lightly toasted almonds and oats.

SERVES 4

3 Navel oranges (or mix of citrus including pink Navels, clementines, grapefruit or blood oranges)
50g (1¾oz) caster sugar

Supreme the citrus following the instructions on page 59. Bring a kettle or a small pan of water to the boil, then pour 25ml (1fl oz) water over the sugar and stir until the sugar is completely dissolved. Allow the sugar syrup to cool completely before proceeding.

Using a small sharp knife like a paring knife, segment the citrus over another small bowl, allowing the slices of fruit to fall into the bowl along with any juices (see page 59). Remove any pips with the tip of your knife. Once all the segments have been carved out, take the leftover citrus membrane and squeeze the remaining juice through a sieve into a separate bowl. Measure the citrus juice and add the same amount of sugar syrup to the juice.

Pour the liquid over the segments of citrus and leave them to marinate for 30 minutes before serving.

VARIATIONS
Grapefruit: Double the amount of sugar for the sugar syrup and allow the segments to marinate for 1 hour before serving.

Clementine and Blood Orange: Instead of segemnting the fruit, slice it into pinwheels. Add one extra citrus for the juice.

Candied Citrus Peel

Candied citrus peel is one of those treats I never fail to make every year. It's budget-friendly, adaptable, and once you grasp the technique, it becomes remarkably simple. Similar to making jam, I find that candying peel at home is easier to handle when done in small quantities. Plus, once you understand the underlying process, you won't necessarily require a recipe. Here I have provided a set of informational guidelines, rather than precise instructions. This means you can candy any variety of citrus, in any quantity you desire, whenever the mood strikes you.

a single type of citrus
equal parts of water and
    sugar by weight
glucose (optional)

Juicing: Slice the citrus across the equator, then extract the juice, using a juicer or press. Whichever method you use, try not to apply too much pressure, which could damage the pith or tear the skins. Save the juice for another purpose, like sorbet (page 49).

Blanching: Blanching the peel helps to extract the bitterness in the pith. To blanch, place the citrus cups into a pan and fill with enough cold water to submerge the fruit. Place over a high heat and bring to a rolling boil. Immediately remove from the heat and strain. Working quickly, place the cups back into the pan and cover with cold water again. Continue blanching in this way, using the table below as a guide:

FRUIT	NUMBER OF BLANCHES
ORANGES	4 blanches
BLOOD ORANGES	4 blanches
GRAPEFRUIT	7 blanches
YUZU	5 blanches
LEMONS	4 blanches
MEYER LEMONS	2 blanches
TANGERINES	3 blanches

Boiling: Boiling the fruit fills the cell walls with water, softening the peels and preparing them for candying. During the final blanching stage, lower the heat and simmer until the pith becomes tender. You will know the pith is ready when you can effortlessly pierce it with your fingernail. Carefully strain the hot liquid and set the peel aside to cool.

Scooping and slicing: The soft inner pith gives the final candied peel its pleasantly bitter taste and soft, chewy texture. Once the citrus cups are cool enough to handle, use the edge of a metal spoon to scoop out the inner membrane of the peel without removing too much pith. After removing the membrane, slice the peel into long strips about 5mm (¼in) thick.

Syrup: Boiling the strips in a sugar syrup replaces the water in the peel with sugar, which sweetens and preserves it. Prepare enough syrup to fully submerge the peel, allowing enough space for the syrup to reduce and thicken. Make the syrup by combining equal parts of water and sugar. If using glucose, add 1 tablespoon of glucose for every 500ml (18fl oz) of syrup. Warm all the ingredients together until the sugar and glucose are completely dissolved, then let the syrup cool to room temperature.

The moment you've been waiting for... Candy time!: Place the strips of peel into a heavy-based saucepan and pour the room temperature syrup over them until the fruit is completely submerged, with an additional 5cm (2in) or so of syrup. This extra liquid will allow the syrup to reduce, and ensures the peel will cook evenly. Cover the fruit with a piece of baking parchment and bring to the boil. Drop the heat to a simmer and observe the bubbles for a minute or so, looking out for a champagne simmer (page 28). Check regularly to make sure the syrup doesn't boil too rapidly. The cooking time varies depending on the batch size and temperature. For example, a batch of 250g (9oz) of blood orange peel will take about 5 hours to candy over a gentle heat. To avoid overcooking, monitor the peel regularly. Keep a small plate in the freezer, and when you want to check for doneness, place a piece of peel on the plate and freeze it for 1 minute. When the peel appears glossy and translucent, and the chilled syrup feels thick (but not hard), the peel is ready. Allow the peel to cool in the syrup, then remove it with a fork, tongs or a slotted spoon, letting the excess syrup fall away. Arrange the peel in rows on a wire rack to dry for a few hours or overnight. Once dry, coat them in caster sugar and store in an airtight container.

Serving suggestions: Use to decorate Little Chocolate Pots (page 145), Ginger Cake (page 90), Lemon Curd Tart (page 39), Honey Lavender Ice Cream (page 164) or a Chocolate Tart with Marsala Sabayon and Toasted Hazelnuts (page 192). Sprinkle over Blood Oranges in Caramel (page 50), Roasted Rhubarb (page 75) or Macerated Strawberries (page 100). Serve them with the Clementine Sorbet (page 49), the Lemon Ice Cream (page 37) or with a Strawberry Sorbet (page 102) and Rosé Jelly (page 195).

Seville Orange Marmalade

Of all the delicious and exciting marmalades in the world I always come back to this classic one made with Seville oranges. It is more work than the average jelly or jam, but that work pays off with glistening jars of bittersweet marmalade to smear on buttered toast, fold into cakes and present to worthy friends. Marmalade is easily found in the average grocery store, but none of the jars on those shelves are ever like the ones made at home.

MAKES 6 x 250G (9OZ) JARS

Day 1
1kg (2lb 4oz) Seville
   oranges
2.5 litres (4½ pints) water

Day 2
1.75kg (3lb 13oz) caster
   sugar
juice of 1 lemon

NOTES:
Allowing the skins to properly simmer in the water will soften them. This gives the final peels a glossy and translucent pith. The pips add pectin, while the lemon juice increases the acidity. Together they assist with the set, so it is worth including them in the recipe. I like to add the sugar to the Seville orange mixture after it has boiled. I find it sets much quicker, thus retaining the brighter flavours of the fruit.

Wash the Seville oranges under cold water, rubbing your fingers against the skin to remove any dirt. Pat them dry, then cut each orange in half across the equator. Squeeze the bitter juice and pips into a bowl, then place a sieve over another bowl and strain the juice from the pips, but do not discard the pips or the juice. Trim a piece of muslin large enough to comfortably enclose the pips and tie with string. Set it aside in a clean bowl or on a small plate.

Using the edge of a metal spoon, scoop out the inner membranes of the oranges while keeping the white pith intact. Discard the membranes and transfer the peel to a cutting board. With a long, sharp knife, slice the peel into long strips as thin as possible. If you can visualize 3mm (⅛in), then aim for that, otherwise go as thin as you can without cutting your fingers.

In a large stockpot (about 10 litres/17½ pints), combine the orange strips, juice, water and the muslin containing the pips. Bring to the boil, then reduce to a simmer and cook for 2–3 hours until the peels are soft and translucent. Remove from the heat and allow the liquid to cool to room temperature. I use an enamel pot and leave the mixture on the work surface overnight, but you may choose to transfer it to a non-reactive container and store it overnight in the refrigerator.

The following day, remove the muslin and wring out any liquid inside. Heat the whole mixture over a medium heat until it begins to boil. Stir in the sugar and lemon juice and bring back to the boil before reducing the heat slightly. Cook for 20–30 minutes, or until the marmalade is set. To check the set, place a small spoonful of marmalade on a chilled plate and place back into the freezer. After 1 minute, run your finger through the marmalade, the liquid should begin to wrinkle, but only slightly. Don't worry too much if the marmalade doesn't hold right away, it will continue to set in the jars as it cools.

Recipe continued overleaf

Seville Orange Marmalade

Carefully remove the pot from the stove and allow the marmalade to settle for 10 minutes. Ladle into hot sterilized jars and close the lids, but instead of placing the filled jars back in the oven, leave them to cool at room temperature overnight, trying not to disturb the liquid. The next day, check the jars have sealed, then tighten the lids and store properly. (See Notes on Making Jam, page 107.)

VARIATIONS

Seville Orange and Oloroso Marmalade: Add 175ml (6fl oz) smooth, slightly aged Oloroso sherry once the marmalade is off the heat. Stir and let the pot sit for 10 minutes before ladling into jars.

Blood Orange and Passion Fruit Marmalade: Replace the Seville oranges with 1kg (2lb 4oz) blood oranges. No need to remove the pith. Simply cut the blood oranges into thin pinwheels and remove any pips. Place into a stockpot with the water and bring to a simmer. Proceed with the recipe as above. Add 350g (12oz) sieved passion fruit with the sugar and continue to cook until set.

HOW TO SUPREME AND SEGMENT CITRUS

Supreming citrus is the process of slicing the white pith and peel away from the fruit. From there you may choose to slice the citrus into pinwheels (for blood oranges and clementines) or segment the citrus by slicing it away from the fibrous walls (for Navel oranges and grapefruits). When it comes to supreming and segmenting citrus, I find that using a sharp, freshly honed blade is essential. A sharp edge will slice rather than tear through the fruit, providing clean wedges that won't fall apart. Try to maintain the natural round shape of the fruit and remove as little of the flesh as possible. Supremed citrus can be refrigerated for up to a day, but sliced pinwheels or segments will maintain their integrity for only a couple of hours.

To supreme, trim off the top and bottom of the citrus peel. You only need to remove enough peel to expose the flesh slightly. This will help to stabilize the citrus on the chopping board and guide your knife between the flesh and the pith. Stand the citrus upright on the board and, starting where the flesh meets the peel, gently use a back-and-forth motion to slice the pith away from the flesh. Follow the natural shape of the fruit, tilting the knife to maintain its rounded form. Continue until all the pith has been removed. Any remaining white pith can be trimmed at the end. Once you are finished, the fruit can be covered and stored in the refrigerator for up to a day.

To segment, take the supremed fruit into your hands and, working over a bowl, slice towards the centre along the white membrane until you reach the core. Next, slice along the adjoining membrane to release the segment, allowing it to fall into the bowl along with any remaining juices. Using a knife in this manner requires care to protect yourself from injury. So, remain focused, work at a steady pace and avoid applying too much force. If you prefer an extra level of caution, then lay the citrus on its side onto a chopping board, slice the segments and transfer them to a bowl as you go. The remaining membrane should still have plenty of juice, so squeeze out the excess juice before dicarding.

Almond Marmalade Cake

Tender, perfumed and not too sweet, here is a cake for any time of the day. Enjoy lightly toasted with butter for breakfast or brunch. Serve with tea in the afternoon, or dress it up in the evening with poached kumquats and softly whipped cream scented with Grand Marnier. And, because the cake is made with ground almonds, it stays moist and tender for several days. If the cake begins to dry out after a few days, simply enliven it in a hot pan with a slice of butter and eat warm with another spoonful of marmalade over top. This recipe is a keeper.

SERVES 8–10

2 small jars of marmalade (about 240g/8½oz total)
165g (5¾oz) caster sugar
55g (2oz) icing sugar
90g (3¼oz) ground almonds
140g (5oz) soft unsalted butter, cubed, plus extra for greasing
190g (6½oz) eggs (about 4 medium eggs)
zest of 1 small orange (or lemon if you like)
1½ teaspoons amaretto or Grand Marnier
90g (3¼oz) plain flour, plus extra for dusting
1 teaspoon baking powder
½ teaspoon salt

NOTES:
For a stronger, sweeter flavour, add more marmalade or chopped candied peel. For a grown-up flavour, use the Seville Orange and Oloroso Marmalade (page 58).

Preheat the oven to 160°C/325°F/gas mark 3. Grease a 900g (2lb) loaf tin with butter, then dust with flour. Tap to remove the excess flour and line the bottom of the tin with baking parchment.

Scoop the marmalade into a heavy-based saucepan and place over a low heat. Warm the marmalade to loosen its consistency without bringing it to the boil, then strain the marmalade through a sieve and place the jelly back into the saucepan. When the peel is cool enough to handle, finely chop it and set aside.

Using a food processor, grind the sugar, icing sugar and ground almonds. Add the cubes of butter, then continue to mix until the batter is very smooth and fluffy. Follow with the eggs, one at a time, pulsing the machine until each egg is absorbed before adding the next. Open the machine and scrape the sides of the bowl using a spatula. Blend until the eggs are absorbed and the mixture looks smooth and glossy. Add the orange zest and amaretto then blend until combined.

In a small bowl, whisk together the flour, baking powder and salt. Add half the flour mixture to the batter and pulse the machine a few times. Add the rest and mix until no dry patches remain. Finally, scatter the chopped fruit and gently mix to combine.

Scrape the batter into the tin and bake for 45–55 minutes, or until a skewer comes out clean. Remove the cake from the oven and cool in the tin on a wire rack.

Once the cake is room temperature, return the pan of marmalade jelly to the heat to gently warm through. Avoid getting the marmalade too hot here, it should be thick and syrupy, but pourable. Remove the almond cake from the tin and generously brush the top with the marmalade, applying several coats and allowing the marmalade to fall down the sides of the cake. Leave to cool completely before serving. This will store in an airtight container for up to 5 days.

Almond Marmalade Cake

Sea Bass in Fish Broth with Lime and Coriander

This dish benefits from its own subtlety. A mild-flavoured fish is poached in a delicate broth, perfumed with lime and coriander. The resulting dish is straightforward with all of the flavours clearly projected.

SERVES 4

For the fish broth
500g (1lb 2oz) white fish bones
1 tablespoon olive oil
1 medium leek, chopped
½ fennel bulb, chopped
¼ white onion, chopped
1 celery stick, chopped
1 teaspoon salt
½ teaspoon whole black or white peppercorns
1 fresh bay leaf
200ml (7fl oz) dry white wine

For the sea bass
a bunch of fresh coriander
600g (1lb 5oz) small potatoes
about 1 litre (1¾ pints) fish broth (see above)
4 fresh sea bass, fileted with skins on and bones removed
4 limes
salt and pepper

The night before remove any veins or remaining skin from the fish bones. Cut or chop them to fit into a container, then submerge them completely in ice-cold water, cover and refrigerate overnight.

The following day, in a large stockpot, gently warm the olive oil over a low heat. Add the leek, fennel, onion, celery, salt, peppercorns and bay leaf. Stir until the ingredients are well coated with the oil, then cover and let them simmer for 10–15 minutes, stirring occasionally to prevent browning.

Meanwhile, drain the liquid from the fish bones and rinse them under cold water until the water runs clear. Set aside. Once the vegetables are softened and translucent, turn up the heat to medium–high and add the white wine. Bring to the boil and continue to stir until the wine evaporates. Add the fish bones and about 1½ litres (2½ pints) of water. Give the stock a gentle stir, then cover it with a lid and heat to a champagne simmer (page 28) for 30 minutes. Ladle through a fine-mesh sieve or a colander lined with a piece of muslin into a heatproof bowl. Use immediately or store in the refrigerator for up to 3 days.

For the sea bass, pick the delicate coriander leaves and reserve the stems. Place the leaves in a small bowl, then cover with damp kitchen paper and store in the refrigerator. Boil a pan of salted water and cook the potatoes until tender. Drain and set aside. Pour about 1 litre (1¾ pints) fish broth into a separate large pan and add the coriander stems, along with the zest of 1 lime. Bring to a simmer then slip the fillets of sea bass into the broth. Cover with a lid, then reduce the heat slightly and poach for about 3–4 minutes until the fish is just set in the centre. Meanwhile, supreme the zested lime following the instructions on page 59, then segment the flesh into a small bowl.

To serve, slice the potatoes and arrange into four individual bowls followed by the sea bass. Squeeze the juice of 1 lime into the broth, then strain into a jug and equally distribute between the bowls. Scatter with the segments of lime and fresh coriander leaves. Serve with more wedges of lime on the side.

Early Spring Salad of Pink Navel Orange, Sugar Snap Peas, Fennel, Avocado and Feta

This salad perfectly demonstrates how to balance sweetness with acidity, and crunchy with creamy. Its flavours remind me of early spring in California.

SERVES 4–6

1 head of Romaine or
    2 heads of Little Gem
    lettuce
1 pink Navel or other large
    orange
200g (7oz) sugar snap peas
1 fennel bulb
150g (5½oz) feta, crumbled
1 avocado
4 tablespoons Simple
    Vinaigrette (page 148)
salt and black pepper

Separate the leaves from the lettuce, removing any damaged ones, and wash under cold water, then lay them on kitchen paper to dry completely. Supreme the orange (see page 59) and slice into segments. Squeeze the juice from what remains from the citrus membrane, then add 1 teaspoon of the citrus juice to the Simple Vinaigrette.

Trim the sugar snap peas and cut into half diagonally, then place into a large bowl. Peel away the tough outer layers of the fennel bulb and reserve them for something else like fish broth (page 62). Thinly slice the fennel using a mandolin or sharp knife and add to the bowl with the sugar snap peas.

Toss the fennel and snap peas with half of the vinaigrette, then add the lettuce and toss again. Very gently fold in 100g (3½oz) of the feta and half of the orange. Using a metal spoon, scoop out segments of avocado and add them to the salad. Taste, adjust with salt and pepper, and add a dash more vinaigrette if the salad feels underdressed. Carefully transfer to a wide plate or shallow bowl, and top with the remaining avocado, orange, feta and a drizzle of vinaigrette.

VARIATIONS
Swap the pink Navel orange for thin wedges of sweet grapefruit or add razor-thin pinwheels of kumquats. If fresh citrus is out of season, but the peas and fennel are still tasting sweet, then serve this salad with fresh, pitted cherries.

Poached Kumquats

In this recipe, thin slices of kumquats are lightly simmered in a sugar syrup until their centres turn translucent. When kumquats are ripe, they taste like nature's sweet and sour candy. However, if the raw kumquat's bitterness is too sharp for your liking, a simple poach is just enough to smooth out its edges. Here I find the secret to success lies in using a very sharp knife. A clean cut will provide neat little pinwheels that maintain their shape both before and after cooking.

SERVES 10–12

300ml (10fl oz) water
225g (8oz) caster sugar
300g (10½oz) kumquats, completely orange in colour

Pour the water and sugar into a saucepan, gently warming it until the sugar dissolves. Remove the pan from the heat and set aside.

Using a very sharp knife, slice the kumquats into thin pinwheels about 2mm (⅟₁₆in) thick. As soon as you encounter a pip, stop slicing and use the tip of the knife (or a prong of a fork) to pluck it out. If you wait until after having sliced all the fruit, you'll be faced with the tedious task of picking out slivers of pip in every slice.

Add the kumquats to the poaching liquid and return the pan to the heat. Bring to a boil, then reduce the heat to a champagne simmer (page 28) for 10–20 minutes. Remove the pan from the heat and allow the kumquats to cool in their liquid. Transfer to a non-reactive container, such as glass, and store in the refrigerator. They will keep in the refrigerator for 2 weeks or more, but if you wish to store them for longer, transfer them while hot into sterilized jars (see Notes on Making Jam, page 107), and keep them in the refrigerator for up to a month.

When you are ready to use the kumquats, lift each slice out of the syrup with a fork and give it a little tap on the side of the container, allowing the excess liquid to drain off.

Serving suggestions: Serve with Little Chocolate Pots (page 144); Almond Marmalade Cake (page 60); Ginger Cake (page 90); Lemon Curd Tart (page 39); Honey Lavender Ice Cream (page 164) or Chocolate Tart with Marsala Sabayon and Toasted Hazelnuts (page 192). Fold them through Blood Oranges in Caramel (page 50), Roasted Rhubarb (page 75) or Macerated Strawberries (page 100). Serve them with the Clementine Sorbet (page 49), the Lemon Ice Cream (page 37) or with a Strawberry Sorbet (page 102) and Champagne Jelly (page 195).

IN THE WORDS OF THE FARMER

Giovanni and Asunta Bernabei

Bernabei Farm, Italy, Citrus

Forty-one years ago we established the Bernabei Farm as part of our family's pursuit of wholesome food. From the beginning, the farm has championed environmentally-friendly farming methods, achieving official organic certification in its tenth year.

Situated in the Lazio region, within the province of Frosinone in the lower Ciociaria, the 6-hectare (15-acre) farm dedicates itself to horticulture, fruit production and the harvesting of wild species. Historically, this region was part of the Terra di Lavoro province whose inhabitants were known as *Terroni*, due to their profound connection to the land.

Seasonal rhythms are the heartbeat of our small family farm, driving a rich biodiversity, both cultivated and wild. A considerable number of the varieties we plant are ancient and native, having evolved over time to prosper together in the local environment. This adaptation is crucial for ensuring a consistent and high-quality yield.

Sustaining soil fertility is also pivotal for stable, high-quality production. Not only do we utilize organic fertilizers, as sanctioned by organic agriculture standards, but we also pay meticulous attention to the way we treat the soil. This involves rotating plots of land and allowing them to lie fallow, thereby enhancing the soil's organic matter. For pest control, we rely on Mother Nature, resorting to organic farming-approved products only when pathogens or parasites significantly threaten our crops.

Throughout the farm we grow many varieties of fruit: mandarins take the spotlight, followed by lemons, oranges, persimmons, plums, apricots, pomegranates, figs and prickly pears. One particular variety of mandarin that we love is the Miyagawa mandarin. It's the first citrus fruit of the season, anticipating oranges and clementines by several weeks. It's small and firm, with a smooth, shiny green peel that is unbelievably aromatic when grated. The thing I like most about the Miyagawa is the rustic nature of the plant: it's one of the most resistant to low temperatures compared to other citrus fruits, and results in a late flowering that is generally unaffected by late frosts. It has great adaptability to the soil, and when it's in flower the scent is so intense that it stays on you even after 12 hours. The plant, when loaded with ripe, beautiful fruit, looks like a decorated Christmas tree. The fruit is seedless, with bright orange flesh and a flavour that is sweet, floral and somewhat bitter, ending with a note of grapefruit. This mandarin is enjoyed for the whole year as *Marmellata di mandarini* (mardarin marmalade), and especially around harvest time as *Mandarini e fagioli al insalata*, a green bean and mandarin salad.

Over fifteen years ago, Alice Waters and Mona Talbott approached us to supply fresh produce to the American Academy in Rome. Chefs from the Academy regularly visit our farm, and a portrait of Giovanni, drawn by a former fellow, hangs on the kitchen wall, accompanied by his personal manifesto for all to read. Every Sunday we travel to the Academy, where kitchen interns collect and meticulously store our produce for use the following day. On these days, we also sell our goods at the farmers' market at Città dell'Altra Economia. At the Academy, preparing and cooking our vegetables straight from the farm can be labour-intensive for novice chefs. However, this practice fosters a deeper connection between them, our work, and the vibrant land.

We firmly believe that cultivating and producing food is a means of safeguarding the environment and preserving the land for future generations of farmers.

Translated by Sarah Levi

Citrus

GOOD SOIL = GOOD FOOD

Many people would agree that fresh seasonal food which comes from rich, healthy soil is better for you and the planet. Nobody understands this better than the farmers who steward the land and grow regeneratively. Healthy soil promotes better water retention and biodiversity. It is nutrient rich and doesn't have to rely on chemical inputs to ward off disease. This type of farming practice aims to improve, revive and regenerate the land. We must do our best to support farmers who work to rebuild our degraded soil and grow quality produce, so that they in turn may support us with a thriving planet.

Furthermore, soil that is rich and fertile grows food that is both healthy and delicious. Such food inspires us and strengthens our connection to the natural world. Good food and good farming are inextricably linked. In fact, it is hard to know when the farmer's work ends and the cook's work begins. Each is equally responsible for the creation of delicious food.

'The health of soil, plant, animal and man is one and indivisible.'

Lady Eve Balfour, *The Living Soil*, 1943

Vin d'Orange

This refreshing, highly drinkable aperitif hails from Provence, France. I've been making it for over 15 years and enjoyed countless variations including swapping the bitter oranges for grapefruit, or the white wine for rosé. I admit this recipe makes quite a large batch, but when the dog days of summer are upon you, the bottles will disappear fast. That said, the recipe can be easily adjusted to a more manageable volume.

MAKES ABOUT 5 X 75CL (26FL OZ) BOTTLES

5 Seville oranges
1 sweet orange
1 lemon
3 litres (6⅓ US pints)
    dry white wine, such
    as Sauvignon Blanc
500ml (18fl oz) vodka
500g (1lb 2oz) sugar
1 vanilla pod, split

Rinse the citrus thoroughly, running your fingers along the knobbly skin to remove any dirt, then pat dry and set aside. Slice the fruit into thick pinwheels (about 4–5 pinwheels per fruit), discarding any pips.

Place the wine, vodka, sugar and vanilla into a 5-litre (10½-US pint) glass jar and stir with a non-metal spoon to dissolve the sugar. Add the fruit and stir once more, then place a large ceramic plate over the fruit to keep it submerged. Seal and store in a cool, dark space for 4–6 weeks. Light and warmth can damage the properties of wine, so it is best to find a place with a cool stable temperature.

Every week for a month, give the vin d'orange a gentle stir to increase the wine's contact with the fruit. Taste after 4 weeks and if the flavour is to your liking, strain and decant into bottles. If not, check every few days until you are satisfied with the intensity of the bitter oranges.

To bottle the vin d'orange, first pass the mixture through a strainer and discard the fruit. Ladle the remaining liquid through a fine-mesh sieve lined with muslin, then funnel into bottles. I try to avoid the sediment at the bottom to retain clarity, but if this feels wasteful to you, strain the last bit through a double-lined muslin. Once bottled, return the vin d'orange to a cool, dark place for an additional 3–4 months. This duration is perfect for allowing you to enjoy the first bottle with the arrival of the summer sun. When stored properly, vin d'orange will keep, mellow, and even improve with age. Serve well chilled, over ice.

VARIATIONS
Vin de Pamplemousse: Replace the Seville oranges with 4 large fragrant grapefruits.

Mixed Citrus: Replace the Seville oranges with 4 blood oranges and use 2 lemons. If you can find it, add ½ bergamot, otherwise add a small lime. Continue with the recipe as above.

Vin d'Orange

STALKS & SHRUBS

RHUBARB, BLACKCURRANT, GOOSEBERRY

Fruits of the *Ribes* genus (gooseberries and currants) may possess little
genetic resemblance to rhubarb, but they all share a special place in the
canon of British cooking. Revered for their tart, earthy and often vegetal
flavour, these fruits require a considerable amount of sugar (and often
cream) to make them palatable in desserts. It's worth noting that despite
being technically classified as a vegetable, rhubarb has long been treated
as a fruit in culinary practices. That being said, their lack of natural
sugars means gooseberries, currants and rhubarb lend themselves
to many savoury dishes, especially ones with fish, duck or pork.

Rhubarb heralds spring, followed by gooseberries in early summer.
Red, white and blackcurrants are ready to harvest by midsummer, and
if the weather is mild, blackcurrants will produce through August. In the
UK, rhubarb is also grown in sheds throughout winter and harvested by
candlelight. Producing rhubarb in the dark results in it growing thinner,
sweeter stems. The tradition dates back to the late 1800s and it is still
practised today in Yorkshire's famous Rhubarb Triangle. Their electric
pink stalks add a splash of colour to winter dishes at a time when all
other British fruit-bearing plants lie dormant.

RHUBARB PAIRINGS

NUTS	*Almond, hazelnut, macadamia*
FLOWERS, LEAVES AND HERBS	*Elderflower, orange blossom, rose, angelica, chervil, sweet cicely*
SPICES	*Cardamom, ginger, vanilla*
FRUITS	*Apple, blood orange, coconut, raspberry, Seville orange, strawberry*
VEGETABLES	*Beetroot, cabbage, fennel, pea, spring onion*
FLOURS	*Buckwheat, oat, spelt*
WINES	*Muscat dessert wine, sparkling wine, vin d'orange, Vin Santo*
DAIRY, MEAT AND FISH	*Buttermilk, cream cheese, crème fraîche, mascarpone, yoghurt, pork, oyster, salmon, shellfish*
OTHER FLAVOURS	*Honey, vinegar*

FAVOURITE COMBINATIONS WITH RHUBARB

STRAWBERRY • ROSE | MUSCAT DESSERT WINE • CREAM | APPLE • GINGER
ALMOND • BUCKWHEAT | BLOOD ORANGE • BUTTERMILK | CARDAMOM • YOGHURT
OYSTER • CRÈME FRAÎCHE | SALMON • CHERVIL

Roasted Rhubarb

When cooking rhubarb, there is really no need to add water. All the liquid required is naturally stored within the stalks. By macerating the stalks in sugar, we can draw out their natural juices and soften the fibres. The final cooked rhubarb is glossy and tender, with a pure, undiluted flavour.

SERVES 4–6

450g (1lb) rhubarb,
  trimmed
225g (8oz) caster sugar
½ vanilla pod, split
1 tablespoon cornflour
zest and juice of ½ orange
  (optional)

Rinse the rhubarb under cold water and pat dry. Slice the stalks into sticks about the length and width of your index finger. Toss with 150g (5½oz) of the sugar, then place into a container and store in the refrigerator overnight.

The following day, preheat the oven to 180°C/350°F/gas mark 4.

Remove the rhubarb from the refrigerator and lay the rhubarb in rows in a ceramic roasting tray just large enough for them to sit snugly. Take a spatula and scrape any residual sugar and juice over the rhubarb.

Put the remaining sugar into a bowl and scrape the seeds from the vanilla pod into the sugar. Use the tips of your fingers to distribute the vanilla, then add the cornflour and whisk everything together. Scatter the sugar over the rhubarb and, if you are using the orange, add the zest and juice now. Cover with foil and bake for 20–25 minutes until the rhubarb is tender, but still holding its shape. Cool on a rack to room temperature. If placed in a well-sealed container, roasted rhubarb will keep for 4 days in the refrigerator.

Rhubarb and Brown Butter Tart

Making this tart involves several components, but many can be prepped ahead of time to simplify the process. A portion of the rhubarb is pre-cooked and strained, enabling more fruit to fit into the final tart. The extracted liquid is then reduced to a luscious glaze.

SERVES 10–12

26cm (10¼in) tart tin,
  lined with 1 quantity of
  flaky pastry (page 218)
  and chilled
1 quantity Roasted
  Rhubarb (page 75)
1 teaspoon cornflour

For the filling
20g (¾oz) plain flour
20g (¾oz) almond flour
40g (1½oz) caster sugar
1 egg
4 teaspoons whole milk
25g (1oz) brown butter
  (see page 230)

For the topping
400g (14oz) rhubarb
55g (2oz) caster sugar

To serve
Macerated Strawberries
  (page 100)
vanilla ice cream

Preheat the oven to 180°C/350°F/gas mark 4.

Keep the flaky pastry tart case chilled until you are ready to assemble and bake the tart. (Preferably well wrapped in the freezer, otherwise, in the refrigerator.) Place a colander over a bowl and transfer the roasted rhubarb to drain. Use a spatula to scrape all the delicious juices from the pan, avoiding any bits that may have burned, then set aside.

To make the filling, whisk the plain flour into a bowl and add the almond flour and sugar, whisking to combine. Whisk in the egg and milk. Brown the butter following the method on page 230, then slowly whisk into the filling. Set aside to cool completely. This can be done up to 2 days in advance and stored in the refrigerator.

Slice the raw rhubarb into quarters, then slice the stalks into long strips about the thickness of your index finger. Place into a bowl and toss with the sugar.

When you are ready to assemble the tart, remove the pastry-lined tin from the freezer. Spread the brown butter filling across the bottom of the tart, followed by the strained rhubarb (reserving the liquid for the glaze). Lay the raw rhubarb over the top of the filling and slide onto a rack in the middle of the oven. Bake for 25 minutes, then carefully rotate the tart. If the top looks like it is beginning to brown, loosely cover with a piece of baking parchment and continue cooking for another 30–40 minutes until the pastry is golden and the filling begins to sink slightly.

While the tart is baking, make the rhubarb glaze. Place the reserved juices from the roasted rhubarb into a pan with the teaspoon of cornflour. Stir to dissolve the cornflour, then place over a medium heat and simmer until the sauce thickens slightly. Remove from the heat and cool to room temperature.

Transfer the tart from the oven onto a wire rack and brush with some of the glaze. Allow it to cool completely. This tart is best served several hours out of the oven to allow the filling to set and the rhubarb to reabsorb its juices. Glaze once more just before serving. Serve with macerated strawberries and vanilla ice cream.

Rhubarb and Brown Butter Tart

Buckwheat and Almond Muffins with Rhubarb

Buckwheat is not actually a wheat – or even a grain – but rather belongs to the knotweed family along with rhubarb. It seems to make sense, then, that buckwheat and rhubarb have a natural affinity for each other, despite the strong vegetal flavour they both have. Combined here they make a wholesome muffin with the addition of ground almonds and yoghurt, which provides an extra-tender crumb.

MAKES 12 MUFFINS

100g (3½oz) spelt flour

100g (3½oz) buckwheat flour

175g (6oz) ground almonds

1 teaspoon baking powder

½ teaspoon bicarbonate of soda

3 eggs

400g (14oz) caster sugar

½ teaspoon salt

340g (11¾oz) whole yoghurt

20g (¾oz) unsalted butter, melted

200g (7oz) rhubarb, chopped into 3cm (1¼in) pieces, then roasted according to page 75

demerara sugar, for sprinkling

Preheat the oven to 170°C/340°F/gas mark 3½. Line a 12-hole muffin tray with paper muffin cases.

In a medium bowl, combine the flour, buckwheat, ground almonds, baking powder and bicarbonate of soda and whisk to combine everything.

In a separate bowl, add the eggs, sugar and salt. Whisk until the eggs are light and satiny and have tripled in volume. Fold in the yoghurt and melted butter, followed by the dry ingredients. Finally, fold through the roasted rhubarb. Some of the rhubarb may fall away into the batter but gentle folding will leave some streaks of rhubarb suspended in the batter.

Spoon the batter into the muffin cases and generously scatter the tops with demerara sugar. Bake for 15–20 minutes until the tops are lightly golden and a toothpick inserted into the centre comes out clean. Cool on a wire rack and serve slightly warm. These will keep in an airtight container for 3 days.

Slow-cooked Salmon with Pickled Rhubarb Relish

This recipe embraces rhubarb's natural tartness and is best served with a weighty fish like salmon or spooned over oysters as a dressed-up mignonette sauce.

SERVES 4

1kg (2lb 4oz) side of
salmon, skin on, bones
removed
2 tablespoons olive oil
salt and pepper
aioli (page 44), to serve

**For the pickled rhubarb
relish**
2 thin stalks of rhubarb,
or 1 thick one
200ml (7fl oz) red wine
vinegar
100ml (3½fl oz) water
1½ teaspoons salt
50g (1¾oz) caster sugar
1 bay leaf
2 teaspoons coarse ground
mustard
4 tablespoons olive oil
20g (¾oz) flat-leaf parsley
leaves
20g (¾oz) another soft
herb, such as chervil,
fennel or dill

Rinse the stalk(s) of rhubarb under cold water and remove the tops just under the leaves and the tough bits near the ends. Dry, then finely dice the rhubarb and transfer to a heatproof bowl. Combine the red wine vinegar, water, salt, sugar and bay leaf in a pan and place over a gentle heat. Bring the pickling liquid to just under the boil, then pour over the rhubarb and leave for 15 minutes.

In a separate bowl, whisk together the mustard and olive oil. Finely chop the herbs and add to the oil. When the rhubarb is ready, strain away the poaching liquid and remove the bay leaf. Add the pickled rhubarb to the herby oil and gently fold the ingredients together, taking care not to bruise the herbs. Taste and adjust with more vinegar or salt if necessary.

Preheat the oven to 120°C/250°F/gas mark ½. Line a high-sided tray with baking parchment and lay the salmon skin-side down. Drizzle the top of the salmon with olive oil and season generously with salt and pepper. Bake for 35–45 minutes until the edges begin to turn opaque and the thickest part of the flesh is easily pierced with a fork. Remove from the oven and allow the fish to rest for a few minutes.

To serve, cut the fish into portions and remove the skin. Spoon the rhubarb relish over the top and serve with a bowl of aioli on the side.

BLACKCURRANT & GOOSEBERRY PAIRINGS

NUTS	*Almond, hazelnut, walnut*
FLOWERS, LEAVES AND HERBS	*Elderflower, rose, rose geranium, bay leaf, blackcurrant leaf, lemon verbena*
SPICES	*Anise, black pepper, ginger, vanilla*
FRUIT	*Blackbery, lemon, lime, raspberry, strawberry*
VEGETABLES	*Beetroot, cucumber, fennel, spring onion*
FLOURS	*Corn, khorasan, oat, rye, spelt*
WINES AND SPIRITS	*Muscat dessert wine, sparkling wine, Vin Santo, rum*
DAIRY, MEAT AND FISH	*Buttermilk, comté, cream, cream cheese, mascarpone, ricotta, yoghurt, beef, chicken, duck, pork, mackerel*
OTHER FLAVOURS	*Chocolate, coffee, honey*

FAVOURITE COMBINATIONS WITH GOOSEBERRY & BLACKCURRANT

BLACKCURRANT • ROSE GERANIUM | BLACKCURRANT • DUCK • BLACK PEPPER

BLACKCURRANT • BEETROOT • RICOTTA | BLACKCURRANT • GOAT'S CHEESE • RYE

GOOSEBERRY • ELDERFLOWER • LEMON | GOOSEBERRY • LEMON VERBENA • YOGHURT

GOOSEBERRY • STRAWBERRY • ALMOND | GOOSEBERRY • SPRING ONION • MACKEREL

Blackcurrant Conserve with Rose Geranium

The first time I arrived at Ballymaloe Cookery School in Cork, Ireland, I had the privilege of dining with Tim and Darina Allen at their house. That meal remains etched in my memory: delectable lobster vol-au-vents accompanied by freshly picked salad leaves, Tim's homemade cheese with brown bread and a rose geranium posset paired with blackcurrants and sugared biscuits. The memory of it inspired this recipe.

A conserve is a loose jam, with shreds of fruit still intact. I often prefer them to jams with a firmer set because they require less sugar and result in a brighter flavour. The late addition of rose geranium in this recipe tames the blackcurrants' slight astringency. The perfume from the rose geranium, in turn, is balanced by the vividly flavoured currants. When at all possible, pick the rose geranium just before cooking (the plant is a hardy perennial that grows well in a window box). This is a great breakfast condiment, whether spooned onto toast or swirled into yoghurt. Alternatively, you can fold it into a medley of other summer berries and serve it alongside cake and crème fraîche. Or add a spoonful into the base of a flute glass, along with cassis (blackcurrant liqueur) and top up with champagne, for an extra-fancy Kir Royale.

MAKES 4 x 450G (1LB) JARS

1 kg (2lb 4oz) topped and tailed blackcurrants
700g (1lb 9oz) caster sugar
2–4 fresh rose geranium leaves, stems removed

Place the blackcurrants into a heavy-based pan with 150ml (5fl oz) of water and cover with a lid. Cook over a medium–high heat until the currants begin to burst, then add the sugar. Stir to incorporate the sugar using a spoon or spatula to gently bash the fruit. Bring the mixture to the boil, then reduce the heat to a simmer. Meanwhile, place a small ceramic plate into the freezer. Run a spoon or spatula along the bottom of the pan, making sure the fruit doesn't stick, then continue to let it simmer away, stirring occasionally. Allow it to cook for 15 minutes, then gently crush the rose geranium leaves in your hand and stir into the blackcurrants. Cook for another 5 minutes or so.

To check if the conserve is set, place a small spoonful on the chilled plate and place back into the freezer. After 1 minute, run your finger through the jam; if it wrinkles, it is ready. Remove the pan from the heat and let the conserve settle for 5 minutes. Remove the rose geranium with a fork, then ladle the conserve into hot sterilized jars. (See Notes on Making Jam, page 107.)

VARIATIONS
Instead of rose geranium, try using 7–10 lemon verbena leaves, or 1 tablespoon of high-quality rose water or 1 split vanilla pod with its scraped-out seeds added along with the sugar. Or simply omit the additional flavouring altogether.

Stalks & Shrubs

Blackcurrant Jelly

In this recipe, the blackcurrant is set with gelatine rather than pectin, resulting in a bright, fresh-tasting jelly which can be served with a number of dishes both savoury and sweet. It is one of my favorite accompaniments to a number of cheeses, like a young moussey goat's cheese or a creamy blue. You may also consider serving small spoonfuls with a terrine or duck pâté on toast. For a sweeter alternative, serve with cold thick cream and Sugared Rose Petals (page 116) or include as a layer in your favourite summer trifle. This jelly should be quivering when set, and barely held together by the gelatine. To achieve this, pay particular attention to your measurements.

SERVES 6–8

570ml (19fl oz) blackcurrant juice (see below)

150–200g (5¼–7oz) caster sugar, plus extra to taste

4 sheets of gelatine leaf

Measure 100ml (3½fl oz) of the blackcurrant juice into a small saucepan with the sugar. Place over a gentle heat, swirling occasionally until the sugar dissolves and the juice is hot to touch, then set aside.

Meanwhile, submerge the gelatine sheets one by one into a bowl of ice-cold water and leave to soften for about 5 minutes. Remove the gelatine from the cold water and squeeze to remove the excess liquid, then add it to the warm currant juice and stir until the gelatine is completely dissolved. Slowly stir in the remaining juice, then strain through a fine-mesh sieve into a bowl. Give the jelly a little taste and add a whisper of sugar if desired. Place into the refrigerator uncovered for 2–3 hours, then cover and continue to chill until set.

You may also set the jelly in ramekins, which can be turned out onto a plate after a quick dip into hot water.

BLACKCURRANT JUICE

MAKES ABOUT 600ML (20FL OZ)

700g (1lb 8oz) topped and tailed blackcurrants

200ml (7fl oz) water

Place the blackcurrants in a saucepan with the water, then cover the pan with a lid and bring it to a gentle boil. Lightly mash the currants and let them cook for an additional minute. Remove from the heat and carefully strain the juice through a fine-mesh sieve into a heatproof container. Use the back of a ladle to gently press the fruit, being cautious not to agitate it too much to avoid clouding the juice. Use immediately, or cover and store in the refrigerator for up to 3 days.

Pan-fried Duck Breast with Blackcurrants and Black Pepper

At the wonderfully inventive, now closed, restaurant Relæ in Copenhagen, I experienced a seven-course meal thoughtfully paired with housemade juice instead of wine. I vividly recall a perfectly cooked duck served with a glass of blackcurrant juice and black pepper. The juice echoed the flavours of Syrah from Northern Rhône in France, a wine classically paired with duck. The pairing, to my mind, was thoughtful and clever cooking at its best.

SERVES 4

4 duck breasts
250g (9oz) topped and
   tailed blackcurrants
20g (¾oz) caster sugar
5 black peppercorns
1 tablespoon balsamic
   vinegar
olive oil
salt and pepper

Before you begin cooking, bring the duck breasts up to room temperature.

Combine the blackcurrants with 50ml (1¾fl oz) of water in a saucepan and put it over a medium–high heat until the blackcurrants begin to release their juices. Strain the mixture, reserving the berries, and return the juices to the heat. Add the sugar, peppercorns and a pinch of salt, and simmer for 10 minutes until the juices turn dark and glossy, and you can see your reflection in the pan. Remove the peppercorns with a slotted spoon, add the berries and simmer for 5 minutes, then turn off the heat, leaving the warm sauce in the pan.

Preheat the oven to 200°C/400°F/gas mark 6. Place the duck breasts on a chopping board and lightly score the skin without penetrating the flesh. Make 2–3 scores in a long diagonal direction, then 2–3 scores in the other direction forming a diamond pattern. Lay the breasts skin-side down into a cold, ovenproof cast-iron pan, then cook over a medium–low heat for 8–10 minutes, undisturbed, until the skin begins to crisp. The fat will render into the pan helping to brown the skin. Resist the temptation to move the duck until the skin easily releases from the pan. You may need to do this in two rounds if the pan seems crowded.

Meanwhile, make two little boats out of foil, just large enough to cradle two duck breasts each. Set aside in a warm place. Once the duck skin releases easily from the pan and has turned a dark golden brown, transfer the pan to the oven for 1–2 minutes, just long enough for the heat to touch the top of the breast. Remove the breasts from the pan and season with salt and pepper, then transfer them to the foil boats, skin-side up. Let them rest for 7–10 minutes before slicing.

Warm the blackcurrant sauce and add the balsamic vinegar and any remaining juices from the resting duck. Slice the warm duck breasts and fan onto plates. Spoon the blackcurrant sauce over the top and finish with freshly cracked black pepper.

Pan-fried Duck Breast with Blackcurrants and Black Pepper

IN THE WORDS OF THE FARMER

Jane Scotter

Fern Verrow, England, Blackcurrants

The higher-than-average rainfall in the Black Mountains of Herefordshire, England, where my farm, Fern Verrow, is situated, is well-suited to the production of blackcurrants. I have been growing a range of seasonal soft fruits for the past thirty years and I can honestly say my blackcurrant bushes have never let me down, and in many summers have been outstanding in both the quantity and quality of the fruits they have borne. The first buds can appear as early as March and are followed by blossoms (of the early season variety) in early April – adorable little pink-blushed, pixie-hat-shaped flowers. The lush, fragrant green leaves follow soon after. This is the time when we hope for April showers to set the fruit and to keep the skies cloudy, reducing the likelihood of frost. A late spring frost can easily damage the delicate flowers and therefore threaten the promise of bounty.

Once the little green berries appear there is little to do but wait for the fruit to gradually turn to a dark, inky black, which usually starts in late June or early July. It is best to wait to harvest the berries until the pearl-like clusters are at least eighty per cent black.

Blackcurrants are mostly puréed for ice cream or sauces, so a few soft stalks are not a problem, but for crumbles, tarts etc you will have to top and tail each berry; a fiddly job that takes time and makes a suitable task for a group of people and good conversation. Tedious or not, it is always worth the effort, they really are the most delicious berry.

As with all currants, we prune and tend to the bushes in early autumn by removing weak or damaged branches and tips. I like to prune with a bowl shape in mind, keeping the middle open to allow good air circulation. I remove branches that may cross and touch others. On older plants, to encourage new growth I often remove one or two older branches. Some time before Christmas, I apply a generous collar of manure or rich compost around the base of the plant, avoiding the crown so as not to inhibit any new growth or encourage any mould or rot that may develop in the wetter months. This timely feeding of the plant is directed to the roots, so that they may be strong and in turn the plant is refreshed and well fed to develop healthily in the spring.

Fern Verrow is a certified biodynamic farm. Biodynamic growing and farming is essentially an organic approach to growing food, meaning that the use of chemical fertilizers and pesticides are prohibited. Biodynamics does however take this a little further. If you like, it is a holistic way of looking at food production, not only looking at the tangible realm of the soil, but also the unseen forces and energies of life and growth that permeate all living things.

Ginger Cake with Gooseberries and Lemon Cream

This cake delivers on all levels. It's altogether light and sticky with a fiery kick from the ginger. It comes together quite effortlessly, and the addition of treacle and oil means you can enjoy it for several days. The flavours go particularly well with gooseberry and lemon, but this cake can serve as a vehicle for any number of the fruits in this book, some of which I have mentioned below.

SERVES 10–12

For the cake
300g (10½oz) plain flour, plus extra for dusting

½ teaspoon ground cinnamon

½ teaspoon ground cloves

½ teaspoon salt

120g (4¼oz) fresh peeled ginger (weighed after peeling), sliced into coins

200g (7oz) caster sugar

230ml (8fl oz) grapeseed oil (or other neutral oil)

240ml (8½fl oz) boiling water (measure after it has been boiled)

2 teaspoons bicarbonate of soda, sifted

260g (9½oz) black treacle

120g (4¼oz) eggs

For the lemon cream
100g (3½oz) Lemon Curd (page 38)

60ml (2fl oz) cold double cream

Sweet Gooseberry Compote (page 94), to serve

Preheat the oven to 140°C/285°F/gas mark 1. Grease and line a 23cm (9in) cake tin.

Sift the flour, cinnamon, cloves and salt into a large bowl. Place the ginger and sugar into a blender and whizz into a paste. If the ginger is still chunky, drizzle in a couple spoonfuls of the oil until everything is nice and smooth, then turn off the motor.

Boil a kettle of water, and then measure 240ml (8½fl oz) into a saucepan. Bring the water back to the boil in the pan, and as the water is boiling, add the bicarbonate of soda. Swiftly remove from the heat and pour the hot water into the blender with the motor off. Add the treacle and oil, then use a wooden spoon or spatula to stir the hot water, loosening the treacle. Blend on the lowest setting for a few seconds. Make a well in the centre of the flour, and slowly pour the wet ingredients into the dry, whisking from the centre outwards until all the flour is drawn in, then whisk in the eggs.

Pour the batter into the lined tin and level the surface.

Bake for 25 minutes, turn the cake and bake for another 25 minutes. Increase the oven temperature to 160°C/325°F/gas mark 2 and bake for a further 10–15 minutes until the centre is done – a skewer or toothpick inserted into the centre should come out clean. Cool in the tin on a wire rack. To serve, run a knife under hot water before slicing.

For the lemon cream, whisk the lemon curd to loosen it. Whip the double cream to stiff peaks, then fold in the lemon curd. Taste and add a little sugar if needed. Serve the cake with a spoonful of lemon cream and gooseberry compote.

Serving Suggestions: Serve with Macerated Strawberries (page 100) and mascarpone cream, Peaches in Syrup (page 162) with softly whipped cream, Poached Pears (page 30) with crème fraîche or Citrus in a Lightly Sweetened Citrus Juice (page 51) with Lemon Cream (above).

Ginger Cake with Gooseberries and Lemon Cream

Mackerel with Gooseberry Compote and Yoghurt

Mackerel and gooseberry are a classic and reliable pairing. Make this in the earlier part of summer when the gooseberries are at their peak.

SERVES 4

4 fresh mackerel, gutted
olive oil
salt and pepper

To serve
Savoury Gooseberry
   Compote (page 95)
thick full-fat yoghurt or
   crème fraîche

Heat a cast-iron frying pan, or equivalent pan, over a high heat. Lightly score the mackerel skin, then season both sides with salt and pepper. Swirl a spoonful of olive oil around the pan and carefully place the mackerel into the sizzling oil. Cook the fish for 2–4 minutes until the edges are opaque and the skin is crisp. Using a flat metal spatula or long palette knife, turn the fish over and gently press the flesh into the pan. Turn off the heat and allow the fish to continue cooking in the residual heat of the pan.

Serve the mackerel immediately on individual plates, with a spoonful of savoury gooseberry compote and a dollop of yoghurt.

Gooseberry Compote Two Ways

I enjoy a gooseberry compote where the fruit is barely collapsed, marinating in a glossy sauce infused with aromatics like lemon or vanilla. In the recipe that follows, gooseberries are heated briefly to release some of their juices while preserving their shape. The gooseberries are then strained and the liquid is returned to the heat with sugar and aromatics where it is cooked down until fragrant and syrupy. The cooked gooseberries are reintroduced into the pot, gently warmed, and allowed to rest, giving the flavours a chance to harmonize and meld.

SERVES 4

SWEET

500g (1lb 2oz) fresh
   gooseberries, topped and
   tailed
75–100g (2½ –3½oz)
   caster sugar
zest of 1 lemon
½ vanilla pod (optional)

Place the gooseberries into a heavy-based pan with just enough water to come 2–3cm (¾–1in) up the side of the pan. Put a colander over a wide bowl and set aside somewhere within reach. Seal the pan with an airtight lid and place over a medium–high heat. Cook for 2–3 minutes until the pan begins to steam and some of the fruit begins to break down but the majority remains whole. Remove from the heat and tip into the colander, allowing the juices to drain.

After a few minutes, put the fruit into a separate bowl and put the juices back into the pan with the sugar, lemon zest and vanilla, if using. Bring to the boil, then reduce to a simmer and cook for 10–15 minutes until the mixture thickens slightly. Return the gooseberries to the pot and give it a gentle stir, then remove from the heat. Allow it to cool to room temperature before serving. This will keep well covered in the refrigerator for 5 days.

VARIATIONS

Substitute the vanilla with 1 large clean elderflower head or 6 leaves of lemon verbena. Or omit the vanilla altogether and swap the lemon zest for lime. When the compote has cooled, fold in 400g (14oz) strawberries, quartered and lightly macerated in sugar.

SAVOURY

500g (1lb 2oz) fresh
  gooseberries, topped and
  tailed
½ teaspoon grated fresh
  ginger
pinch of salt
25g (1oz) caster sugar
zest of 1 lemon

Place the gooseberries into a heavy-based pan with just enough water to come 2–3cm (¾–1in) up the side of the pan. Put a colander over a wide bowl and set aside somewhere within reach. Seal the pan with an airtight lid and place over a medium–high heat. Cook for 2–3 minutes until the pan begins to steam and some of the fruit begins to break down but the majority remains whole. Remove from the heat and transfer the gooseberries to the colander, allowing the juices to drain.

After a few minutes, put the fruit into a separate bowl and put the juices back into the pan with the grated ginger, salt, sugar and lemon zest. Bring to the boil, then reduce to a simmer and cook for 10–15 minutes until the mixture thickens slightly. Return the gooseberries to the pot and give it a gentle stir, then remove from the heat. Allow it to cool to room temperature before serving. This will keep well covered in the refrigerator for 5 days.

VARIATIONS

Add additional spices like coriander, mustard seeds and fresh green chilli (deseeded and finely diced). Or omit the ginger and add a sprig of tarragon or 1 bay leaf.

Gooseberry Compote

BERRIES

STRAWBERRY, LOGANBERRY, RASPBERRY, MULBERRY,
BLACKBERRY, BLUEBERRY

When seeking out berries, look for the ones that are coloured all the way through. They should be plump and soft, yet retain their shape. If possible, shy away from mushy berries and promptly discard any that show signs of mould before they spoil the rest. I make the effort to buy berries at the farmers' market, or directly from farms where I can be sure they have not travelled far. Unfortunately, berries found in supermarkets are often bred for durability rather than flavour; they can either be hard and sour, or sweet and insipid, but rarely harmonious and enticing. Given their fragile nature, it is best to use them soon after they've been picked. If you need to store them, store them in the refrigerator. Prepare a plate or small tray lined with kitchen paper and scatter the berries in a single layer. Discard any that are mouldy or damaged. Gently cover them with another piece of kitchen paper or a light cloth before storing on a flat surface in the refrigerator. Additionally, many berries can be successfully frozen – see Notes on Freezing Fruit (page 115).

STRAWBERRY PAIRINGS

NUTS AND SEEDS	*Almond, macadamia, peanut, pine nut, pistachio, sesame*
FLOWERS, LEAVES AND HERBS	*Elderflower, rose, rose geranium, anise hyssop, bay leaf, chamomile, lemon verbena, sweet cicely, angelica, mint, sweet marjoram*
SPICES	*Cardamom, ginger, peppercorn, ras el hanout, saffron, vanilla*
FRUITS	*Berry, coconut, gooseberry, kumquat, lemon, lime, loquat, mango, melon, passion fruit, rhubarb*
VEGETABLES	*Fennel, lettuce, pea, tomato,*
FLOURS	*Einkorn, khorasan, oat, polenta, rye, semolina, whole spelt*
WINES AND SPIRITS	*Muscat dessert wine, port, red wine, sparkling wine, white vermouth, white wine, amaretto, brandy, pastis, rum*
DAIRY	*Burrata, buttermilk, cream cheese, crème fraîche, goat's curd, goat's milk, mascarpone, ricotta, sheep's milk, yoghurt, young robiola*
OTHER FLAVOURS	*Balsamic vinegar, coffee espresso, honey*

FAVOURITE COMBINATIONS WITH STRAWBERRY

RHUBARB • CRÈME FRAÎCHE | SPELT • MASCARPONE | GOOSEBERRY • ELDERFLOWER
MELON • ROSE | COFEE ESPRESSO • RICOTTA | COCONUT • LIME
OAT • ALMOND | MINT • LEMON

Strawberries with Warm Spelt Madeleines

I was born in California in the middle of May, and somewhere in a dusty old photo album is a picture of my twin sister and me on our first birthday, peering over a sponge cake adorned with strawberries and cream. As an adult, whenever I spot strawberries at the market, I can't help but yearn for this alluring trio of flavours.

SERVES 4

You will need 16 madeleine moulds

For the madeleines
45g (1½oz) wholemeal spelt flour
80g (2¾oz) plain flour, plus extra for dusting
1 teaspoon baking powder
120g (4¼oz) unsalted butter, plus extra melted, for greasing
15g (½oz) dark brown sugar
10g (¼oz) honey
10g (¼oz) black treacle
165g eggs (3 eggs)
1 teaspoon salt
100g (3½oz) caster sugar

For the whipped cream
200ml (7fl oz) cold double cream
15g (½oz) sugar
½ vanilla pod, split and seeds scraped out

To serve
1 batch Macerated Strawberries (page 100)
icing sugar, for dusting

The day before you plan to bake the madeleines, prepare the batter. Sift both flours and the baking powder together into a bowl. In a small saucepan, heat the butter, brown sugar, honey and black treacle until everything is melted. Remove from the heat and set aside to cool slightly. Meanwhile, place the eggs, salt and sugar into the mixing bowl of a stand mixer and whisk for 7–10 minutes until light and doubled in volume. Remove the bowl from the mixer and gently fold in one-third of the dry ingredients. Follow with the remaining dry ingredients, then slowly drizzle in the butter mixture over the top of the batter. Fold everything together until just combined. Transfer the batter to a sealed container and refrigerate overnight.

The next day, preheat the oven to 170°C/340°F/gas mark 3½. Prepare the madeleine moulds by brushing them generously with melted butter. Apply two coats of melted butter to each mould, then lightly dust with flour and set aside.

Prepare the macerated strawberries using the instructions on page 100.

Remove the batter from the refrigerator and place 1–2 tablespoons of cold batter into each mould. Bake for 7 minutes, then rotate and bake for another 5–6 minutes until the madeleines have puffed up and turned golden.

While the madeleines are in the oven, make the whipped cream by combining the sugar and vanilla seeds in a bowl and rubbing them together using your fingers. Add the double cream and whip to soft peaks, then transfer the cream to a serving bowl. Place the macerated strawberries into another serving bowl.

Once the madeleines arc baked, carefully unmould them by turning the tray upside down and tapping the side against a clean work surface. Arrange the madeleines on a plate, dust with icing sugar and serve warm alongside the strawberries and cream.

Macerated Strawberries

SERVES 4

300g (9oz) strawberries
  (about 1 punnet)
½ tablespoon sugar
½ teaspoon lemon
  or redcurrant juice
  (optional)

Begin by hulling the strawberries (see below) then slice them according to size and place them in a bowl. Large strawberries should be quartered, while smaller strawberries look quite cute when sliced in half. The smallest ones can be left as they are. Personally, I like to envisage a size that can easily be scooped up with a spoon. Scatter the sugar over the strawberries and gently fold everything together, taking care not to damage the delicate fruit. Leave the bowl at room temperature for anywhere from 10–20 minutes. More delicate varieties like French Gariguettes or Mara des Bois will soften in a matter of minutes, whereas sturdier types will benefit from a longer maceration. Taste the berries, and if they seem to call for more acidity, add the lemon juice or redcurrant juice. Adjust the sugar to your liking, then leave for a further 5 minutes before serving.

HOW TO HULL A STRAWBERRY

Hulling a strawberry removes the green stem and flavourless white flesh surrounding it without sacrificing the whole top of the fruit. This technique not only preserves the strawberry's natural shape but also minimizes waste. To begin, use a small paring knife or tourné knife, and position the tip just beneath the stem where the white flesh meets the red. Insert the knife at an angle and turn in one direction, while simultaneously rotating the strawberry in the opposite direction. Pull away the calyx, then use the knife to trim any remaining pale flesh around the top of the strawberry.

Strawberry Sorbet

Like the Clementine Sorbet (page 49), this recipe requires no more than fruit and sugar. To make things easier, you can hull the strawberries ahead of time and keep them refrigerated until you're ready to start churning, then quickly blitz all the ingredients together. This ensures the freshest and most vibrant flavour.

SERVES 8–10

800g (1lb 12oz) ripe,
   perfumed strawberries
70g (2½oz) caster sugar
1 tablespoon lemon juice

Begin by hulling the strawberries (see page 100), then place them in a food processor along with 10g (¼oz) of the sugar. Blitz until the mixture is smooth. If the seeds are quite big, pass the purée through a fine-mesh sieve and reserve half the seeds for later use. Stir in the remaining sugar and the lemon juice. When the sugar has dissolved, taste the purée and adjust the sweetness and acidity to your liking. If desired, stir in the reserved seeds. Churn the mixture in an ice-cream maker following the manufacturer's instructions.

Serving suggestions: Serve with a Coconut Meringue (page 117) or Rosé Jelly (page 195). For a refreshing treat, serve in small, chilled glasses with champagne or sparkling water with muddled mint and lime.

VARIATIONS
Use this method for a raspberry or blackberry sorbet, increasing the sugar to 75–100g (2½ –3½oz), depending on the tartness of the berries.

Strawberry Sorbet

Berries

Mint Ice Cream with Strawberries

Mint is a vigorous and often invasive plant. I find the best time to make this ice cream is in early to midsummer, while the mint is flourishing in the garden but still tender and sweet. Luckily for us, that coincides with the peak of strawberry season, seeming to confirm the old adage 'What grows together, goes together.' This recipe requires a lot of fresh mint, so it is great for when you need to cut back the stems or uproot those pesky shoots. However, don't wait until the plant is completely overgrown or it will taste woody and bitter.

SERVES 10–12

950ml (1⅔ pints) whole
  milk
300g (10½ oz) picked mint
  leaves (for steeping), plus
  60g (2¼oz) for blanching,
  weigh after they have
  been removed from
  the stem
150g (5½oz) caster sugar
¼ teaspoon salt
1 tablespoon cornflour
160ml (5½fl oz) double
  cream

To serve
1 batch Macerated
  Strawberries (page 100)
1 batch whipped cream
  (page 99)

Place the milk into a heavy-based pan over a medium–high heat, ensuring you have a slotted spoon within easy reach. While the milk is heating, remove the mint leaves from the stems. If they happen to be dirty, give them a quick rinse under cold running water and spin them dry in a salad spinner. Once the milk has come to the boil, drop a small handful of mint into the pan and stir. Allow it to steep for 30 seconds, then remove with the slotted spoon. Wait until the mixture returns to the boil, then repeat until you have used all the mint. This technique of extracting flavour is akin to steeping tea. You are looking for a quick extraction to pull out the more aromatic flavours before drawing out the bitterness. Once you have added all of the mint, strain the milk and measure again. You should have 800ml (1⅓ pints) of infused milk. If you are low on volume, simply top up with fresh milk.

Decant about a quarter of the milk into a heavy-based saucepan and bring to a simmer. Place the sugar, salt and cornflour into a dish and whisk together. When the milk comes to the boil, add the sugar mixture and whisk until fully dissolved. Continue whisking until the milk thickens slightly. Remove from the heat and gradually add the remaining milk and cream, whisking as you go. Strain the mixture into a glass container and place that container into another bowl filled with ice water, stirring occasionally. Once the base has completely cooled, cover the container and refrigerate it overnight.

When you are ready to churn the ice cream, prepare 60g (2¼oz) of clean mint leaves, removed from their stems. Bring a small pan of water to a vigorous boil and place a bowl of iced water nearby. Plunge half of the mint into the boiling water, making sure all the mint is properly submerged. Wait 5–7 seconds, then quickly transfer the mint into the iced water to stop the cooking. Remove the mint and squeeze out the excess water, then set aside on a plate. Repeat with the remaining fresh mint. Once you have blanched all the mint, place it into a blender with the ice-cream base and blitz thoroughly on the highest setting for 15–20 seconds until the mint is reduced to fine speckles suspended throughout the milk. Taste to adjust the sweetness if needed. To preserve the colour, churn the mixture immediately in an ice-cream maker following the manufacturer's instructions.

Strawberry and Redcurrant Jam

Making jam from strawberries can be a difficult thing to master. The fruit's naturally low pectin and acidity means it must be cooked for a long time before setting, often resulting in a jam that is muddled and caramelized. Luckily, this is where redcurrants come into play. With their high pectin content and vivid acidity, they not only shorten the cooking time but also enhance the strawberry's flavour, bringing it back into focus once again. This is an excellent recipe to have up your sleeve when there is a glut of strawberries at the market. At the height of the strawberry season, farmers will often sell cosmetically damaged fruit at a discount. If you have a good relationship with either your local farmer or greengrocer, consider asking if they can arrange this for you in advance. It not only makes jam-making more economical but also enables farmers to sell more of their produce while reducing waste. A win-win-win situation, if you ask me.

MAKES 5 x 200g (7oz) JARS

600g (21oz) redcurrants, rinsed under cold water
600g (1lb 5oz) hulled strawberries (see page 100)
650g (1lb 7oz) caster sugar
1 tablespoon lemon juice

Rinse the redcurrants under cool water then transfer to a saucepan. Sprinkle a small amount of sugar over the top of the fruit and add just enough water to come 2–3cm (1 ½ in) up the side of the pan. Place the pan over a high heat and cover it securely with a lid. Once the fruit begins to boil, use a whisk or potato masher to crush the fruit until it is fully submerged in its own liquid. Allow it to return to the boil. Let it cook for an additional 3–4 minutes, and then remove the pan from the heat and pass it through a fine-mesh sieve. Use the back of a ladle to press the purée through the sieve, leaving behind only the skins and seeds.

Place the strawberries and sugar into a saucepan and stir to evenly coat the strawberries. Cover the pan and set it aside in a warm spot away from direct heat, allowing the strawberries to macerate for 30 minutes.

Once the strawberries begin releasing their liquid, measure 400 ml (14fl oz) of the redcurrant juice and add it to the pan along with the lemon juice. Set it over a medium-high heat and, when the mixture comes to the boil, reduce the heat slightly to maintain a steady simmer without bubbling over. Continue to cook for 10–15 minutes.

Meanwhile, place a plate into the freezer to chill. Stir the jam every so often to prevent it from sticking, then check the jam's set. Take the chilled plate and spoon a small amount of jam onto it, before placing it back in the freezer. Check after a minute or two by running your finger through the jam. If the surface wrinkles when pushed, the jam is set. A kitchen thermometer should register 105°C (221°F). Ladle into sterilized jars (see Notes on Making Jam, opposite).

NOTES ON MAKING JAM

PECTIN, ACID AND SUGAR

Pectin, when combined with acid and sugar, takes on a gummy texture. Found primarily in fruit cores, pith, skins and pips, it is released from the cell walls as the fruit cooks. Pectin levels are at their highest when fruit is underripe, and reduce as fruit ripens, or is frozen for long periods of time. Acid is naturally found in all fruits and, when making jam, helps to draw out the pectin and prevent crystallization of the sugar. Acid added before cooking will help to draw out the pectin, and when added after the cooking will brighten the flavour of the jam. The main role of sugar is to preserve the fruit and keep it from spoiling. As a general rule, I add a 60% ratio of sugar to fruit by weight. Boiling the fruit and sugar draws out the moisture and will balance the flavour of jams like blackcurrant, gooseberry, marmalade and rhubarb.

SETTING, STERILIZING AND STORING

Setting This is achieved by the harmonious interaction of sugar, acid and pectin. To test, place a ceramic plate in the freezer before you begin. When you think the jam is ready, drop a spoonful onto the plate and place it back into the freezer for 1 minute. Run your finger through the jam and, if it wrinkles when pushed, it is set. If using a thermometer, this will typically happen when the jam reaches 102–105°C (216–221°F).

Sterilizing and filling jars Preheat the oven to 120°C/250°F/gas mark ½. Place clean jam jars and unused lids onto a tray. Make sure they are evenly spaced, then place into the oven for 20 minutes. When the jam is ready, use a ladle or small heatproof measuring jug to pour it into the jars, leaving a 7mm (¼in) gap at the top. Use a jam funnel to avoid spills and wipe the jars with a warm damp cloth. Use a tea towel to lift up the hot lids and screw onto the jars until they are snug, but not tight. (Or you can screw the lid on tight, then give it a quarter turn to loosen.) Return the jars to the oven for 10 minutes, then transfer to a wire rack. Allow the jars to cool completely, preferably overnight. You may hear the jars pop as they cool and seal. Check the jars have sealed properly, then tighten the lids.

Storage Always store the preserves in a cool, dark place. If a jar doesn't seal properly, store in the refrigerator and consume first. A properly sterilized jar of jam will store for at least 6 months and up to a year.

BERRY PAIRINGS

NUTS AND SEEDS	*Almond, hazelnut, peanut, pine nut, walnut*
FLOWERS, LEAVES AND HERBS	*Chamomile, rose, rose geranium, blackcurrant leaf, fig leaf, lemon verbena*
SPICES	*Aniseed, cardamom, cinnamon, fennel, nutmeg, vanilla*
FRUITS	*Apple, coconut, peach, pear, plum, quince, rhubarb, strawberry, melon*
VEGETABLES	*Celeriac, endive, raddichio, sweetcorn, tomato*
FLOURS	*Khorasan, oat, polenta, rye, semolina, spelt*
WINES AND SPIRITS	*Muscat dessert wine, red wine, sparkling wine, vin de pêche, rum*
DAIRY AND MEAT	*Cream cheese, mascarpone, ricotta, duck, pâté, pork, quail, terrine*
OTHER FLAVOURS	*Honey, muscovado sugar*

FAVOURITE COMBINATIONS WITH BERRIES

BLACKBERRY • DUCK • ANISEED | BLACKBERRY • PÂTÉ • BLACK PEPPER | BLACKBERRY • PLUM • ALMOND
LOGANBERRY • RICOTTA • HONEY | LOGANBERRY • PEACH • VIN DE PÊCHE
RASPBERRY • STRAWBERRY • KIRSCH | RASPBERRY • BLACKCURRANT LEAF • RYE
RASPBERRY • HAZELNUT • CREAM

Any Berry Compote

This is hardly a recipe, but rather a loose guideline. Fruit compotes are often made by lightly macerating the fruit in sugar before briefly cooking on the hob. The resulting sauce is a slightly broken-down fruit in syrup. When it comes to ripe berries, however, I keep everything fresh and uncooked. Heat from cooking subdues the zippy, inky acidity that makes fresh berries so appealing. In this recipe, I toss whole blackberries, raspberries and loganberries in a no-heat purée (page 14) and adjust with a whisper of sugar and lemon juice. It goes without saying that this compote is best when the berries are ripe and most flavourful. If the berries are too sharp, consider using them in a semifreddo, sorbet or cordial. Fresh, vine-ripened berries are susceptible to fermentation. If you are not planning on using the compote right away, I would suggest storing it in the refrigerator where it will keep for up to 2 days.

SERVES 4

250g (9oz) single variety or mixture of berries, such as loganberries, raspberries and blackberries

20–50g (¾–1¾oz) sugar, to taste

50–100ml (2–3½fl oz) berry purée (see page 14)

squeeze of lemon juice, dash of kirsch or crème de cassis

Make sure that all of your ingredients are at room temperature. Before proceeding, glance over the berries for signs of dirt or damage, and carefully remove.

Starting with the smallest amount of sugar, sprinkle over the purée and stir until the sugar dissolves. Place the berries in a wide bowl, add the purée, and gently toss with a spoon to evenly coat them. Leave for 10–15 minutes, then taste. Adjust the sugar as needed, and if desired, add a splash of lemon juice, kirsch or crème de cassis.

Serving suggestions: This is a perfect companion to any simple cake, such as the Lemon Drizzle (page 43), Ginger Cake (page 90) or Almond Cake (page 175). Use to zhuzh up the Honey Lavender Ice Cream (page 164) or serve with spoonfuls of Marsala Sabayon (page 192).

Loganberry Jam

We owe a debt of gratitude to the devoted farmers and avid gardeners over the centuries. Their profound understanding of plants, species, cultivating and breeding means we can enjoy new and exciting varieties born from their inquisitive practices. One such marvel is the loganberry. This cross between a blackberry and a raspberry emerged in a private garden in Santa Cruz, California, nearly 150 years ago, and can now be found growing in gardens and farms across the US and UK. When fully ripened, the loganberry has a wine-like juiciness and a lingering acidity. To me, they make one of the finest jams in summer.

MAKES 5–6 x 200G (7oz) JARS

1kg (2lb 4oz) loganberries
600g (1lb 5oz) caster sugar
juice of 1 lemon

Place the loganberries and sugar into a heavy-based pan. Gently mash the loganberries with a potato masher or the end of a rolling pin, and allow them to macerate for 10 minutes. As the berries start releasing their juices, add the lemon juice, then place the pan over a medium–high heat and bring the mixture to a boil. Reduce the heat slightly and continue to cook, stirring occasionally to redistribute the heat and prevent the jam from scorching on the bottom of the pan. Meanwhile, place a plate into the freezer to chill. Continue to cook the loganberries for about 20 minutes until the mixture is glossy and begins to thicken. To check the set, take the chilled plate and spoon a small amount of jam onto it, before placing it back in the freezer. Check after a minute or two, by running your finger through the jam and if the surface wrinkles when pushed, it is set. A kitchen thermometer should register 105°C (221°F). Ladle into sterilized jars (see Notes on Making Jam, page 107).

'Uniformity is not nature's way; diversity is nature's way.'

Vandana Shiva

Loganberry Jam

Raspberry and Vin de Pêche Granita

Having included my recipe for Vin de Pêche (see page 163), I thought it best to share a recipe that cooks with it too. Red wine and raspberries are a classic combination and here they are elevated by the hint of bitter almond from the vin de pêche. This dish has the added value of being quite effortless, requiring less technique and time in the kitchen compared to making an ice cream or semifreddo. Plus, you'll likely have all the necessary equipment on hand. My favourite way to serve this granita is with fresh raspberries and a dollop of soft cream (yes, wine and cream work well here). Alternatively, serve it with fresh peaches in syrup (page 162).

SERVES 8

200ml (7fl oz) water
50g (1¾oz) caster sugar
250g (9oz) raspberries
500ml (18fl oz) Vin de
 Pêche (page 163)

Warm the water with the sugar in a saucepan until the sugar dissolves. Stir in the raspberries, then set the mixture aside to cool to room temperature. Once the raspberries have become soft and tender, lightly mash them with a potato masher or the end of a rolling pin. Next, strain the mixture through a fine-mesh sieve, pressing the raspberries lightly. Stir in the vin de pêche. Transfer to a wide container like a baking tin and place into the freezer. As a helpful tip, keep a whisk and fork in a bowl near the freezer. Every hour or so, take out the granita and give it a quick stir.

After a few hours, delicate crystals will begin to form. Use the fork to chip away at any icy bits forming in the corners, then use the whisk to gently lift the frozen crystals, allowing them to break apart and fall back into the roasting tray. This method of lifting the ice crystals will yield the lightest and flakiest granita.

After approximately 3–4 hours, cover the granita and leave it overnight. The following day, give it another mix with the whisk before serving.

VARIATION
Use a mixture of berries in place of the raspberries, if that is what you have on hand.

Raspberry and Vin de Pêche Granita

NOTES ON FREEZING FRUIT

Start with quality Freezing will preserve the flavour of fruit, not enhance it in any way. By following these guidelines, you will increase your chances of preserving that quality.

Freeze it quickly The faster you are able to get food below 0°C (32°F), the better texture and flavour it will have once it's thawed. To do this, make sure your freezer is set to a low temperature and has ample space for the containers you intend to use. First open-freeze berries, by laying them on trays lined with baking parchment, then transfer them to containers once they are frozen through. Smaller portions will also freeze faster, aiding in preserving the fruit.

Use thawed fruit right away Refreezing previously thawed fruit will dull its flavour and texture. So, plan to freeze portions in an amount you know you will use. Here is where a little planning will pay off down the road. Try portioning enough fruit for a few jars of quick jam, sauce or sorbet.

METHOD 1: LAY OUT ON TRAYS, FREEZE, THEN TRANSFER TO A BAG OR CONTAINER

Pros Locks in freshness, prevents fruit from freezing into a clump, easy to portion.
Cons Takes up more freezer space.
Good for Fresh berries, hulled strawberries, topped and tailed gooseberries, topped and tailed blackcurrants, stemmed red and whitecurrants, cherries (pitted if you plan to use them pitted, otherwise unpitted), sliced stoned fruit or rhubarb (fruit portioned for pies, cobblers or chutneys), whole blueberries.

METHOD 2: ROASTED FRUIT, NO-HEAT PURÉES, OR FLASH-HEAT PURÉES

Pros Takes up less space in the freezer, easy to use once defrosted, reduces oxidation for stone fruit during the freezing/thawing process.
Cons Loses freshness.
Good for Stoned fruit purées, roasted rhubarb, roasted figs, purées for apples, pears, grapes and quinces.

Mulberry Sorbet with Almond Meringues and Sugared Rose Petals

There is an enchanting quality to mulberries that sets them apart from other berries. Once fully ripened, they unveil a distinctly earthy and inky flavour. However, their delicate nature makes them a challenge to store, so ripe mulberries are hard to come by commercially. If you are fortunate enough to taste one picked straight from the tree, like me, you may be seduced by its charm. A ripe mulberry is bound to stain your fingers and, if left for more than a day or two, it will either wither, ferment or develop mould. Fortunately, mulberries freeze exceptionally well (see Notes on Freezing Fruit, page 115). Frozen mulberries can be chopped and scattered over the base of an apple tart (page 218), or blitzed into a sauce to serve with roasted figs (page 24). The flavour can also be preserved in this simple sorbet, which I like to serve with meringues, cream and sugared rose petals.

SERVES 15

For the meringues
95g (3¼oz) egg whites (about 3 eggs)
190g (6½oz) caster sugar
¼ teaspoon vanilla extract
190g (6½oz) whole almonds, toasted and chopped
¼ teaspoon cream of tartar

For the mulberry sorbet
1kg (2lb 4oz) dark, wine-coloured mulberries
50–100g (1¾–3½oz) sugar
squeeze of lemon juice

For the meringues, preheat the oven to 120°C/250°F/gas mark ½. Line 2 trays with baking parchment.

In the bowl of a stand mixer, combine the egg whites and sugar. Place the bowl over a pot of simmering water, ensuring the water does not touch the bottom of the bowl. Stir with a spatula, scraping the sides and bottom of the bowl to prevent curdling, and heat the mixture until it reaches 80°C (176°F) on a sugar thermometer. Remove from the heat and add the vanilla extract, then place the bowl on a stand mixer with a whisk attachment and whip on medium-high speed until the meringue cools to forms stiff, glossy peaks. Next, gently fold in the almonds, then scoop the mixture by the spoonful onto the lined trays. Bake for 20–25 minutes until the meringues are slightly puffed and easily release from the paper. They should be tender and dry on the outside with a soft, marshmallowy centre. Carefully slide the baking parchment from the tray without breaking the meringues and leave to cool on a wire rack before transferring them to a sealed container.

For the sorbet, use a food processor to purée the mulberries with 1 tablespoon of sugar. Set a fine-mesh sieve over a clean bowl and press the purée through the sieve with the back of a ladle. Discard the mulberry seeds. Add 50g (1¾oz) of sugar and stir until dissolved, then add a squeeze of lemon juice. Adjust the sweetness and acidity to your taste, then churn the mixture in an ice-cream maker following the manufacturer's instructions.

For the sugared rose petals

1 egg white

30 fragrant rose petals, unsprayed

a small bowl of caster sugar

To serve

150ml (5fl oz) cold double cream

1 teaspoon sugar

For the sugared rose petals, make sure your hands are clean and dry and keep a towel nearby. Place the egg white into a small bowl and gently whisk them until frothy. Using one hand, drag your index and middle finger along with your thumb through the frothy whites, then pick up a rose petal and gently rub it between your fingers to moisten it. If the petal feels too heavy, dry your finger with the towel and brush away any excess whites. Drop the petal into the sugar, then use your other clean hand to toss and coat it. Tap the petal on the side of the bowl to remove the excess sugar, then place on a wire rack. Repeat this process with the remaining petals, using one hand to coat them in egg white and the other hand to toss them in sugar. It's best to keep the bowls of egg white and sugar separate to avoid creating a sticky mess. However, if your hands become mixed, simply take a break to rinse your hands, wipe them dry and continue. Once you have sugared all the petals, transfer the wire rack to a cool, moist-free place until the petals are brittle and completely dry. They can be stored in a well-sealed container, stacked between pieces of baking parchment, for up to a day.

If the mulberry sorbet seems firm, then place it into the refrigerator for 10 minutes before serving. Softly whip the cream with the sugar and keep cold. Serve the meringues with a generous scoop of sorbet and a light dollop of softly whipped cream, then scatter a couple of sugared rose petals over the meringue and sorbet.

VARIATIONS

The choice of meringue, ice cream/sorbet and fruit is limitless. Here are some of my favourite combinations:

MERINGUE	INSTRUCTIONS	SORBET/ICE CREAM	SORBET/ICE CREAM
BROWN SUGAR	*Replace the caster sugar with 110g (3¾oz) muscovado sugar and 80g (3oz) caster sugar*	*Strawberry Sorbet (page 102)*	*Macerated Strawberries (page 100) and Flash-roasted Blueberries (page 121)*
TOASTED COCONUT	*Replace the almonds with 110g (3¾oz) desiccated coconut, toasted*	*Clementine Sorbet (page 49)*	*Blood Oranges in Caramel (page 50)*
HAZELNUT	*Replace the almonds with 190g (6½oz) hazelnuts, toasted and chopped*	*Loganberry Semifreddo (page 18)*	*Any Berry Compote (page 109)*
PLAIN	*Omit the almonds and proceed with the recipe*	*Lemon Ice Cream (page 37)*	*Candied Citrus Peel (page 54)*

Mulberry Sorbet with Almond Meringues and Sugared Rose Petals

Polenta Olive Oil Muffins
with Blackberries

The combination of polenta and olive oil creates a muffin that is both light and subtly sweet. While blackberries are my preferred choice for these muffins, feel free to use other fruits according to the season. Try roasted rhubarb in spring, nectarines in high summer or poached pears in autumn. During winter, when fresh fruit is scarce, add a dollop of lemon curd or jam. And the good news is most of the preparation can be done in advance. You can mix the batter, ready the muffin tins, and choose the fruit ahead of time. On the following morning, simply fill the moulds, place the fruit on top, and slide them into the preheated oven.

MAKES 12 MUFFINS

140g (5oz) caster sugar
zest of 1 lemon
190g (6½oz) plain flour
70g (2½oz) polenta
2½ teaspoons baking
  powder
1 teaspoon salt
170ml (6fl oz) whole milk
110g (3¾oz) eggs (2 eggs)
100ml (3½fl oz) fruity olive
  oil
400g (14oz) blackberries
coarse demerara sugar, for
  sprinkling

Begin by combining the sugar and lemon zest in a mixing bowl and rub the zest into the sugar to release its aromatic oils. Add the flour, polenta, baking powder and salt, and whisk together. In a separate bowl, whisk the milk and eggs, then as you continue to whisk, gradually drizzle in the olive oil in a steady stream. Make a well in the centre of the dry ingredients and use a spatula to slowly stir the wet ingredients into the dry. Transfer to a sealed container and store in the refrigerator overnight. This allows the batter to rest and hydrate, resulting in a lighter, more tender crumb.

The next day, preheat the oven to 170°C/340°F/gas mark 3½. Line a 12-hole muffin tin with baking parchment or paper muffin cases, then spoon the batter into the muffin tins, filling them about three-quarters of the way up. Press 6–7 blackberries into each cup. Right before baking, scatter a spoonful of demerara sugar over the top of each muffin and bake for 20–25 minutes until the tops are lightly golden and a toothpick inserted into the centre of the muffins comes out clean. Remove from the oven and allow them to cool on a wire rack. Serve warm or at room temperature. If stored in an airtight container, they will keep for up to 2 days.

BLUEBERRY PAIRINGS

NUTS AND SEEDS	*Almond, macadamia, pistachio, pine nut, sesame*
FLOWERS, LEAVES AND HERBS	*Angelica, chamomile, rose, bay leaf, lemon verbena, lemon thyme, thyme*
SPICES	*Black pepper, cinnamon, ginger, nutmeg, vanilla*
FRUITS	*Apricot, coconut, lemon, melon, nectarine, peach, raspberry, strawberry*
VEGETABLES	*Butterhead lettuce, sweetcorn*
FLOURS	*Einkorn, khorasan, oat, polenta, semolina, spelt, white, whole wheat*
WINES AND SPIRITS	*Muscat dessert wine, sparkling wine, white wine, amaretto, Grand Marnier, kirsch, rum*
DAIRY AND MEAT	*Buttermilk, cream cheese, crème fraîche, goat's curd, goat's milk, mascarpone, ricotta, sheep's milk, yoghurt, young robiola, duck, pork*
OTHER FLAVOURS	*Honey*

FAVOURITE COMBINATIONS WITH BLUEBERRY

LEMON • CREAM CHEESE | OAT • CINNAMON | PEACH • ALMOND
STRAWBERRY • KIRSCH | GOAT'S CHEESE • BLACK PEPPER
POLENTA • LEMON VERBENA | OATS • CINNAMON

Flash-roasted Blueberries

The method for this dish is as straightforward as the name suggests. Blueberries are tossed in
a simple sugar syrup and scented with lemon zest, then briefly warmed through in a very hot oven.
This technique aims to soften the raw texture of the blueberries, while deepening their flavour.

SERVES 4

300g (10½oz) blueberries
1 tablespoon water
30g (1oz) caster sugar
1 teaspoon cornflour
zest of 1 lemon, plus juice
of ½
1 tablespoon kirsch
(optional)

Preheat the oven to 220°C/425°F/gas mark 7.

Rinse the blueberries under cool water and remove any that are mouldy or damaged.
Place them into an ovenproof dish large enough for the fruit to lay in a single layer.
Warm the water, sugar and cornflour in a pan over a medium–low heat until the
sugar dissolves, then spoon the syrup over the blueberries. Add the lemon zest, juice
and kirsch, if desired. Give the dish a little shake, then place it into the oven. After 3
minutes, carefully shuffle the dish and make sure the blueberries are not sticking to the
sides. Return it into the oven for another 3–5 minutes. The blueberries are done when
they begin to steam slightly but still hold their shape. While a few may have started
to break down, creating a glossy sauce of indigo blue, the majority of the blueberries
should remain intact.

Remove from the oven and allow the dish to cool slightly. To serve warm, gently shake
the tray to coat the blueberries with the syrup, then carefully spoon over your desired
dish. Alternatively, let them cool to room temperature, then using a flat spatula,
carefully transfer the blueberries to a container and pour the juices over the fruit.
Cover the container and place it in the refrigerator where they will keep for 4 days.
Allow them to come to room temperature before serving.

Serving suggestions: Fold blueberries through lightly Macerated Strawberries (page
100), or spoon over Peaches in Syrup (page 162). Lemon and blueberries are a classic
combination, so serve these with the Lemon Drizzle (page 43), Lemon Curd Tart
(page 39), or Lemon Ice Cream (page 37). You may also enjoy it with the Honey
Lavender Ice Cream (page 164) or the Strawberry Sorbet (page 102).

VARIATIONS
Add 1–2 teaspoons of honey to the blueberries after they come out of the oven and
gently toss to coat them. Alternatively, crush 4–5 leaves of lemon verbena in the palm
of your hand, and add it to the blueberries for the last minute or two of roasting.

Frozen Yoghurt-Honey Parfait with Flash-roasted Blueberries

This frozen parfait is so clean and refreshing, you will want to make it all summer long. My favourite way to serve it is with roasted blueberries.

SERVES 8

400ml (14fl oz) double
cream
70g (2½oz) honey, plus
extra for serving
400g (14 oz) thick yoghurt
lemon juice
120g (4¼oz) caster sugar
60g (2¼oz) egg whites

1 portion of Flash-roasted
Blueberries (page 121)

Measure two pieces of baking parchment, each approximately 40cm (16in) long. Take the first piece and fold the short ends into thirds like a letter. This will give you a long strip of baking parchment. Lightly oil a 450g (1lb) loaf tin and place the long strip of parchment across the middle of the tin. This will serve as handles when you need to release the parfait. Use the second piece of parchment to line the walls of the loaf tin, with plenty of overhang to cover the top. Place the tin into the freezer until you are ready to use.

Whip the cream until the whisk begins to leave tracks, but before it holds soft peaks, then store it in the refrigerator. Stir the honey into the thick yoghurt in a large bowl until it is fully incorporated, then add a squeeze of lemon juice and set aside.

In the bowl of a stand mixer, combine the egg whites and sugar. Place the bowl over a pan of simmering water, ensuring the water does not touch the bottom of the bowl. Stir with a spatula, scraping the sides and bottom of the bowl to prevent curdling, and heat the mixture until it reaches 80°C (176°F). Remove from the heat, then place the bowl on the stand mixer with a whisk attachment and whip on medium-high speed until it cools. Continue whisking until the meringue forms stiff, glossy peaks.

Using a whisk, fold one-third of the egg whites into the yoghurt, switch to a spatula and continue folding in the rest of the egg whites. Take the cream out of the refrigerator and gently whisk until it holds soft peaks. Working quickly but carefully so as to not lose the volume you've created, fold one-third of the cream into the yoghurt mixture. Follow with the remaining cream until everything is incorporated.

Take the loaf tin from the freezer and pour the yoghurt parfait into the tin using the spatula to scrape the bowl clean. Cover with the overhanging baking parchment and place back into the freezer for 5 hours or overnight.

Recipe continued overleaf

Frozen Yoghurt-Honey Parfait with Roasted Blueberries

Ten minutes before you are ready to serve, transfer the parfait to the refrigerator. Just before serving, get a tray or wide bowl and fill with warm water, then dip the tin into the warm water to help release the parfait. Use a towel to remove excess water from the bottom of the tin, then place the serving plate on the top of the tin. Carefully flip the parfait over, gently tugging on the overhanging parchment until it falls onto the plate. If it won't release from the tin, flip it back over and either dip it into the warm water again, or run a knife over the edges of the parfait until it is loose.

Slice and serve with generous spoonfuls of roasted blueberries and finish with another drizzle of honey.

VARIATIONS
Serve this parfait with Macerated Strawberries (page 100), Gooseberry Compote (page 94), Roasted Cherries (page 22), Citrus in a Lightly Sweetened Citrus Juice (page 51) or a scoop of Quince and Calvados Sorbet (page 239).

FRUIT ON THE SIDE

From the Coconut Rum Cake with Peaches (page 161) to the Almond Cake with Greengages and Fennel Cream (page 175), perhaps you've noticed my inclination for serving fruit alongside cake, rather than baking it within. This preference stems from several observations. One is that fruit and cake have different cooking times, which often leads to overbaked (or underbaked) fruit. It's also not uncommon for fruit to sink to the bottom of the tin or release its juices, resulting in a soggy crumb. Keeping the fruit separate allows you to prepare it in a way that truly accentuates its flavour. It also allows you to be generous with the fruit, making sure there is enough fruit for the last mouthful of cake. If you do want to cook fruit into cake, consider using a shallow tart tin, like I did in the Hazelnut and Pear Cake with Espresso (page 228) or press it into the top of muffin batter like the Polenta Olive Oil Muffins with Blackberries (page 119).

Blueberry, Oat and Buttermilk Scones

The addition of fresh fruit to scones is undoubtedly an American novelty, deviating from the traditional British afternoon tea. Yet as a Californian living in the UK, I take delight in this untraditional variation. These scones are made with oat flour, which contributes to their soft texture and delicate crumb.

MAKES ABOUT 12 LARGE SCONES

150g (5½oz) oats, blitzed
  until fine
300g (10½oz) plain flour,
  plus extra for dusting
½ teaspoon salt
1 teaspoon bicarbonate
  of soda
50g (1¾oz) cold butter,
  cubed
30g (1oz) caster sugar
1 small egg
225–260ml (8–9¼fl oz)
  buttermilk, plus extra for
  brushing
200g (7oz) blueberries
demerara sugar, for
  sprinkling

In a mixing bowl, combine the blitzed oats, flour, salt and bicarbonate of soda, whisking them together. Add the butter and use your fingertips to rub it into the flour until the mixture resembles fine breadcrumbs. Add the sugar and mix well. Make a well in the centre of the dry ingredients and add the egg along with 225ml (8fl oz) of buttermilk. To achieve tender scones, take care not to overwork the dough. With your hand in the shape of a claw, stir in the wet ingredients until a shaggy dough forms, adding more buttermilk if the mixture seems dry. Fold in the blueberries.

Transfer the dough onto a floured work surface and lightly knead it before rolling it into a 3cm (1¼in) thick disc. Rest the dough in the refrigerator for 30 minutes, allowing the glutens to relax, the flour to absorb the moisture and the butter within the dough to chill (this will help lighten the texture).

When you are ready to bake, preheat the oven to 200°C/400°F/gas mark 6. Remove the dough from the refrigerator and place it on a floured work surface. Use a 7cm (2¾in) round pastry cutter to cut out the scones and transfer to a tray lined with baking parchment. Bring the leftover dough together and roll a second time. Cut out a few more scones and add them to the tray. Brush the tops with buttermilk and coat with demerara sugar.

Bake for 7 minutes, then rotate and bake for another 6–7 minutes until the scones are puffed and a light golden brown. Remove from the oven and cool on a wire rack for 10 minutes. Serve warm with butter and jam or clotted cream.

VARIATIONS
For orange and currant scones, rub the zest of 1 orange into the sugar with your fingertips. Replace the blueberries with dried currants plumped in Earl Grey tea, then strained. For spelt and date scones, replace the oats with wholemeal spelt flour and substitute pitted and chopped dates for the blueberries.

STONE FRUIT

APRICOT, CHERRY, PEACH, NECTARINE, PLUM, DAMSON, GREENGAGE

The term stone fruit encompasses any fruit that contains a stone or pit within its flesh. For the purpose of this book, I have narrowed this category down to include apricots, cherries, peaches, nectarines and a variety of plums.

These particular fruits seem to favour climates with long, hot summers and cool winters. While we often rely on farmers to provide us with stone fruits, growing your own fruit tree can bring multiple benefits. The blossoms of cherries, peaches and plums in spring can be infused into ice cream and custards or used to create syrups for cakes and cordials. The stones of apricots and plums are particularly fragrant, while the leaves from peach and cherry trees can enhance roasted fruit or to be used to flavour wine. Get creative with cherry or plum leaves by using them as decorative elements for a fruit platter or preserve cherries and cherry leaves in brandy for future use throughout the year.

Stone fruits are best when allowed to mature on the tree, drinking in the nutrients and basking in the warmth of the sun. This is when they achieve that exceptional balance of sweetness and acidity. For this reason, it is worth seeking out stone fruits that are harvested ripe without the need to travel far. In the UK, this is more easily achievable with cherries, plums and even apricots. If you can't source directly from a farm, seek out shops with short supply chains. Many greengrocers who prioritize sourcing high-quality produce should be able to tell you where your fruit is coming from.

APRICOT PAIRINGS

NUTS	*Almond, hazelnut, macadamia, pistachio*
FLOWERS, LEAVES AND HERBS	*Rose, chamomile, elderflower, lemon verbena*
SPICES	*Anise, cardamom, ginger*
FRUIT	*Blueberry, cherry, coconut, lemon*
VEGETABLES	*Rocket, fennel, pea*
FLOURS	*Plain flour, polenta, rice*
WINES AND SPIRITS	*Muscat dessert wine, white wine, amaretto, brandy, kirsch, noyau liqueur*
DAIRY AND MEAT	*Crème fraîche, double cream, mascarpone, soft triple cream cheese, young goat's cheese, chicken, lamb, pâté, terrine*
OTHER FLAVOURS	*Caramel, honey, vanilla*

FAVOURITE COMBINATIONS WITH APRICOT

ELDERFLOWER · CREAM | POLENTA · MASCARPONE | ROSE · ALMOND | HONEY · MUSCAT
LAMB · GINGER | BLUEBERRY · LEMON | PORK TERRINE · WHITE WINE

Quick Apricot Jam

I prefer to make my jam in small batches, a practice I've maintained even during my time in professional kitchens, but especially when I am at home. Making a jam in small batches captures the fresh, unadulterated flavour of a fruit at its prime and is considerably easier to manage on the hob. However, if you feel inclined to triple or quadruple the recipe, that's absolutely fine as well – just divide everything evenly among three or four pans. It may seem like more work, but keeping the batches small reduces the cooking time so the process overall will move along quickly.

MAKES 5 x 250G (9OZ) JARS

2–2.5kg (4lb 8oz–5lb 8oz) apricots
700g–1.3kg (1lb 9oz–3lb) caster sugar
zest and juice of 2 lemons

Slice the apricots in half, remove the stones and reweigh. You should have 1.8–2.3kg (4–5lb) of fruit. Place the apricot halves into a heavy-based pan and scatter 2 tablespoons of sugar over the top. Cover the pan and leave to macerate for 20 minutes.

While the fruit is macerating, extract the apricot kernels, or noyau, following the instructions on page 137.

When the apricots have finished macerating, add the lemon zest and just enough water to cover the bottom of the pan. Cover tightly with a lid and place over a high heat. Stay close by and do not allow the fruit to burn. Once it has come to the boil, lightly bash the fruit with a whisk, allow it to return to the boil, then quickly remove from the heat and transfer to a bowl to stop the cooking.

When the purée is cool enough to handle, pass through a food mill or sieve to remove the skins. Measure the remaining purée and place into a clean heavy-based pan. For every 1kg (2lb 4oz) of fruit, add 600g (1lb 5oz) of sugar. Stir in the noyau. Cook over a medium–high heat, only stirring often enough to redistribute the heat and prevent scorching on the bottom of the pan. Vigorous stirring at this stage releases too much heat, prolonging the cooking time and dulling the flavour. Cook for about 20 minutes until the jam is glossy and begins to thicken. Add the lemon juice and cook for a further 2–3 minutes. To check the set, place a small spoonful of jam on a chilled plate and place back into the freezer. After 1 minute, run your finger through the jam; if it wrinkles, it is ready. Carefully remove the pan from the stove and allow the jam to settle for 5 minutes. Ladle into hot sterilized jars. (See Notes on Making Jam, page 107.)

Variations overleaf

VARIATIONS

Apricot and Elderflower Jam: Omit the apricot kernels (noyau) and add the zest of 1 more lemon to the purée. Add 2 clean, dry elderflower heads to the jam in the last 3 minutes. Pull the heads out before ladling into the jars, leaving some flowers to remain suspended in the jam.

Apricot and Rose Jam: In the last minute or so of cooking, add 2 teaspoons of good-quality rose water, stir and proceed with the recipe.

Apricot and Vanilla Jam: Slice 2 vanilla pods in half and use a knife to scrape the seeds into the sugar before you add it to your apricot purée. Run the knife through the sugar and carefully use your fingers to pull away any of those precious seeds clinging to the blade. Use your fingers to break up the vanilla seeds. Reserve the pods. Add the vanilla sugar to the apricot purée and proceed as above. When it is time to transfer the jam to the jars, place one half of the vanilla pods into each jar, then ladle the hot jam over top.

Stone Fruit

Apricot and Muscat Tart

This dish is inspired by Skye Gyngell's exceptionally delicious Prune and Armagnac Tart. When I was Head Pastry Chef at her restaurant, Spring, I wanted to pull the dish into summer with the addition of brighter, floral flavours. A layer of velvety apricot purée is covered with a baked almond custard, and when it emerges hot from the oven it is showered generously with sweet Muscat dessert wine. The result is this exquisite tart which continues to make an appearance on the menu at the start of every summer. Don't skip the roasted apricots as they bring the whole dish together.

SERVES 10–12

For the shortcrust pastry

125g (4½oz) cold unsalted butter, cubed

250g (9oz) plain flour, plus extra for dusting

3 teaspoons caster sugar

½ teaspoon salt

1 egg, plus 1 egg yolk

For the filling

125g (4½oz) Apricot Purée (see page 134)

150ml (5fl oz) double cream

2 eggs

100g (3½oz) caster sugar

80g (2¾oz) ground almonds

½ teaspoon salt

30g (1oz) unsalted butter, melted

2–4 tablespoons Muscat de Beaumes de Venise

To make the shortcrust pastry, toss the butter with the flour and place into a sealed container and store in the refrigerator. Chill for at least 30 minutes or up to overnight.

Once the butter and flour are properly chilled, remove them from the refrigerator and tip into a food processor along with the sugar and salt. Blitz until the dough is the texture of breadcrumbs. With the motor running, add the whole egg and egg yolk and continue mixing until the eggs are fully incorporated. Tip the dough onto a clean work surface and bring it together with your hands. Shape into a disc, wrap in baking parchment and store in the refrigerator for at least 3 hours, but preferably overnight.

Unwrap the pastry and very lightly dust both sides. Lay the dough between two pieces of baking parchment, then starting from the centre, begin to roll the dough outward. Give the dough a quarter turn and continue to roll, turning and rolling into an even circle that is about 28cm (11in) in diameter. If the dough is hard to roll, leave it on the work surface for 5 minutes to soften. If the dough feels too soft or begins to stick, place it back into the refrigerator before continuing. Take a 25cm (10in) tart tin, remove the top parchment and lightly dust the surface of the dough with flour. Bring the tart tin next to you, then roll the dough onto the rolling pin. Lift the rolling pin over the tart tin, then unroll the dough over it. Use your fingers to press the dough into the base of the tin and evenly up the sides. Trim the edges and put into the refrigerator to chill.

Preheat the oven to 170°C/340°F/gas mark 3½.

Remove the tart from the refrigerator and line with a piece of baking parchment and pie weights, rice or baking beans. Bake for 20–25 minutes until cooked through. Carefully remove the pie weights and parchment and continue to cook the tart shell for 20–25 minutes until golden. Cool on a wire rack.

Ingredients and recipe continued overleaf

To serve
1 quantity of Roasted
  Apricots (page 21)
crème fraîche or softly
  whipped cream

Increase the oven temperature to 180°C/350°F/gas mark 4.

When the tart shell is cool, evenly spread the apricot purée over its base. In a large bowl, combine the double cream, eggs, sugar, ground almonds and salt. Whisk everything together and then gradually incorporate the melted butter. Ladle two-thirds of the filling onto the apricot purée. Carefully place the tart on the middle shelf of the oven. Pour the remaining filling into the tart, then gently close the oven door. Bake for 25–30 minutes until the top is golden brown and the edges are set, but the centre has a slight wobble.

Remove the tart from the oven and lay on a towel or heatproof surface. Drizzle the Muscat de Beaumes de Venise over the surface and allow it to settle for 5 minutes. Transfer the tart to a wire rack and continue to cool completely. This tart is best served at room temperature with 2–3 roasted apricots and a dollop of crème fraîche. Drizzle with the remaining juices from the roasted apricots.

VARIATION
For Skye's original Prune and Armagnac Tart, replace the apricot purée with prune purée and add 1 tablespoon of orange blossom water to the custard. When the tart comes out of the oven, drizzle 3 tablespoons of Armagnac over the top.

APRICOT PURÉE

MAKES 120G (4¼ OZ)

4–5 large apricots, halved
  and stoned
40g (1½oz) sugar

Roughly chop the apricots then place them in a small saucepan with just enough water to cover the bottom of the pan. Cover tightly with a lid and place over a high heat. Stay close by and do not allow the fruit to burn. Once it has come to the boil, lightly bash the fruit with a whisk, allow it to return to the boil, then quickly remove from the heat and transfer to a bowl to stop the cooking.

When the purée is cool enough to handle, pass it through a food mill or sieve to remove the skins. Measure 120g (4¼oz) of purée and add 40g (1½oz) of sugar. Return it to the saucepan and cook for 10 minutes over a medium-low heat until glossy. Remove from the heat and allow to cool.

Noyau Extract

I tend to make this when I have an abundant supply of apricots, but you can also make this towards the end of the apricot season by collecting the kernels, known as noyau, along the way. Simply store the kernels in a small freezer container until you have enough to make a batch. The extract improves as it ages, so I often make a batch one year, then let it mature until the following year. It is great splashed over roasted stone fruit, spooned onto a scoop of vanilla ice cream, or used to flavour cakes.

MAKES 500ML (18FL OZ)

150g (5½oz) apricot
  kernels
500ml (18fl oz) vodka

Preheat the oven to 160°C/325°F/gas mark 3.

Lay the apricot kernels on a wide tray, then place into the oven for 5 minutes. Give the tray a little shake, then rotate and bake for another 5 minutes. You want just enough heat to pass through the kernels to deactivate any harmful compounds, but avoid any darkening of their colour, which would alter their flavour. See page 137, Noyau: Cracking the Stone, for notes on amygdalin.

Once the kernels have cooled, place them into a glass jar and add the vodka. Give it a stir, then seal and store in a dark, cool place. Turn the jar every week for a month, then let it sit for another two months. Strain the liquid through a muslin, then pour into sterilized bottles and continue to age for 3 months before using.

NOYAU LIQUEUR

MAKES 500ML (18FL OZ)

150g (5½oz) apricot
  kernels
500ml (18fl oz) vodka
100g (3½oz) caster sugar
50ml (1¾fl oz) of water

Make the noyau extract according to the recipe above. Once the liquid is strained through a muslin, set aside.

In a small saucepan, add 100g (3½oz) caster sugar with 50ml (1¾fl oz) of water. Bring to the boil, then remove from the heat and cool to room temperature. Add the sugar syrup to the noyau extract, then bottle and store for 1 month, gently turning or swirling the bottle once a week. Continue to age for 2–3 months before using.

Stone Fruit

NOYAU: CRACKING THE STONE

Cracking open an apricot stone can be a slippery and messy affair, sending shrapnels of shell across the room. However, a few clever tricks should ease the process and keep everything contained.

Begin by rinsing the apricot stones and pull away any flesh clinging to them, then pat them dry. Take a tea towel or some kitchen paper and place it horizontally on a sturdy wooden surface or a piece of marble. Arrange the apricot stones in a single layer on the lower half of the towel and fold the top half over to cover them. Using a hammer or rolling pin, gently crack the stones open. Unfold the towel, pull out the white kernels (noyau) and place them into a bowl. When you are finished, take a moment to inhale the aroma from the kernels: they should smell fragrant with the scent of bitter almonds.

It is worth noting that noyau contain amygdalin, a compound that is toxic to humans when ingested in very high doses. Luckily, it is destroyed when exposed to heat, so there is no concern when adding it to recipes like the Quick Apricot Jam (page 129). However, if you plan to use noyau in their raw state, then lay them on a tray and place in a preheated oven at 180°C/350°F/gas mark 4. Bake for 5–10 minutes, then remove from the oven and allow them to cool. Noyau can be frozen and, if well-sealed, will keep for up to 2 months.

Warm Almond-stuffed Apricots with Fior di Latte and Honey

Several years ago I cooked with Alice Waters and the chefs of the Rome Sustainable Food Project at the American Academy in Rome. This initiative aims to teach how to cook simple Italian food guided by principles of sustainability. For a gala event, we showcased Italian loquats, strawberries and cherries. For dessert, we stuffed apricots with almond frangipane paired with Roman honey ice cream. The milk-based ice cream in this recipe brings levity to the baked apricots, making it an ideal summer dessert.

SERVES 4

For the fior di latte
800ml (1⅓ pints) whole milk
160ml (5½fl oz) double cream
150g (5½oz) caster sugar, plus extra to taste
¼ teaspoon salt
1 tablespoon cornflour

For the apricot filling
6 small apricots or 4 large ones
100g (3½oz) almonds, lightly toasted
100g (3½oz) soft amaretti biscuits
60g (2¼oz) caster sugar
1 tablespoon plain flour
100g (3½oz) cold unsalted butter, cubed
1 egg yolk, lightly whisked

mild, good-quality honey, to serve

To make the fior di latte ice cream base, combine the milk and cream in a jug then decant about a quarter of the mixture into a heavy-based saucepan and bring to a simmer. Place the sugar, salt and cornflour into a dish and whisk together. When the milk comes to the boil, whisk in the sugar and continue whisking until it thickens slightly. Take it off the heat, and slowly whisk in the remaining milk and cream mixture. Strain into a container and allow to cool to room temperature. Once fully cooled, cover and refrigerate overnight. The following day, taste the base and add more sugar if desired. Finally, churn it in an ice-cream maker following the manufacturer's instructions.

For the apricot filling, slice the apricots in half and remove the stones. Crack two of the stones to remove the noyau (see page 137). Place the almonds, amaretti biscuits, noyau, 30g (1oz) of the sugar and the flour into a food processor and blitz until fine. Add the cubes of cold butter and continue processing until the the mixture resembles coarse crumbs. Then add the egg yolk and pulse a few times until the mixture looks moist yet crumbly. Transfer this mixture to a bowl.

Preheat the oven to 200°C/400°F/gas mark 6. Arrange the apricots cut-side up into a roasting tray large enough so they are spaced apart. Fill each apricot centre with a small spoonful of the almond mixture. Bake for 15 minutes, then rotate the tray and scatter the remaining 30g (1oz) sugar over the fruit. Continue baking for another 7–10 minutes until the apricots begin to colour around the edges and the almond filling turns golden brown. Remove from the oven and lace a spoonful of honey over the apricots. To serve, arrange the warm apricots in a bowl, add a scoop of the fior di latte ice cream and another drizzle of honey.

VARIATION
As you might expect, any stone fruit can be baked in this fashion. So feel free to swap in peaches, nectarines or plums for this recipe.

CHERRY PAIRINGS

NUTS	*Almond, hazelnut, pistachio, walnut*
FLOWERS, LEAVES AND HERBS	*Rose, cherry leaf, peach leaf, sweet cicely, thyme, bay leaf*
SPICES	*Cinnamon, vanilla, cardamom, toasted anise, black pepper*
FRUITS	*Banana, coconut, apricots, orange*
VEGETABLES	*Fennel, green bean, spinach, lettuce, rocket, pea, cucumber*
FLOURS	*Plain, rye, spelt, wholemeal*
SPIRITS AND WINES	*Red wine, sparkling wine, amaretto, brandy, kirsch, rum*
DAIRY AND MEAT	*Blue cheese, brown butter, buttermilk, Camembert, chocolate, crème fraîche, mascarpone, ricotta, robiola, soft sheep's milk cheese, chicken, duck, pork, squab, terrine*
OTHER FLAVOURS	*Chocolate, coffee, apricot kernels, cherry kernels, muscovado sugar, honey,*

FAVOURITE COMBINATIONS WITH CHERRY

ALMOND • KIRSCH | RICOTTA • HONEY | COFFEE • HAZELNUT | COCONUT • RUM
MUSCOVADO SUGAR • SPELT | RED WINE • DUCK | PISTACHIO • ROSE
CHOCOLATE • AMARETTO | TERRINE • BRANDY | FENNEL • CHICKEN

Cold Cherries and Soft Almond Cookies

I like to serve this in midsummer when light stretches late into the evening and we dine at the garden table. Cherries are one of the few fruits I enjoy served chilled (see more in A Case for Cold Cherries, page 142). Here they sit beside chewy almond cookies. Cherry and almond are distant cousins, and if you pay attention you can taste the almonds in the cherries.

SERVES 4–6

325g (11½oz) ground almonds

50g (1¾oz) brown sugar

250g (9oz) icing sugar, plus extra for coating

½ teaspoon bicarbonate of soda

20g (¾oz) honey

1 teaspoon salt

2 teaspoons almond liqueur, Noyau Extract (page 135) or vanilla

1 whole egg

2 egg whites

NOTE:

This recipe yields more biscuits than you might need. Baked biscuits can be stored in an airtight container for up to 3 days. However, if you choose to freeze the dough, roll it into 20g (¾oz) balls and place in a sealed container layered between baking parchment before storing in the freezer.

Whisk together the ground almonds, brown sugar, icing sugar and baking soda in a bowl. In a saucepan, warm the honey, salt and almond liqueur over a low heat to loosen the honey, then set aside. Stir the egg and egg whites into the dry ingredients, then follow with the honey. (This can also be mixed in a food processor.) When the dough is well mixed, transfer it to a sealed container and store it in the refrigerator overnight.

When you're ready to bake, preheat your oven to 180°C/350°F/gas mark 4. Line a baking tray with either a silicone mat or baking parchment. Sift the icing sugar into a medium bowl, then roll the cookie dough into 20g (¾oz) balls. Squeeze each one to flatten slightly, coat in icing sugar, and arrange them on the prepared tray, pressing them gently with your finger.

Bake the cookies for 8 minutes, then rotate the tray 180 degrees and continue baking for another 6–8 minutes. The cookies should puff up and lightly brown around the edges while maintaining a soft, chewy centre. Once baked, remove from the oven and carefully transfer the cookies to a wire rack and allow them to cool completely. Serve on a plate next to a bowl of chilled cherries (page 142).

A CASE FOR COLD CHERRIES

Most fruits are best enjoyed at room temperature and some, like peaches or raspberries, are enhanced by a touch of warmth from the sun. But there are exceptions to every rule and I find this is the case with cold cherries. The slight chill on a ripe cherry firms the texture and enlivens the flavour, making each bite taste crisp and cool. The juice bursts as it breaks through the skin and the flavour is sharp and more pronounced.

Before serving the cherries, select ones that are firm and deeply coloured. Look for stems that are green and supple, and then leave them intact. Place the cherries on a plate lined with kitchen paper and refrigerate them for at least 30 minutes. If desired, you can also chill the serving bowl. When you're ready to serve, transfer the cherries to the bowl and provide a small plate for discarded stones and stems. On particularly hot summer days, consider placing the bowl of cherries on top of another bowl filled with ice to keep them refreshingly cool.

I like to serve cold cherries with slices of terrine and a leafy salad dressed in a mustardy vinaigrette. At the end of a meal, cold cherries might accompany a creamy sheep's milk cheese or a spicy blue. For a sweet treat, I serve chilled cherries with a plate of Soft Almond Cookies (page 142) and nothing more.

A Case for Cold Cherries

Little Chocolate Pots with Roasted Cherries and Kirsch Cream

Here is a creamy chocolate custard topped with roasted cherries and softly whipped cream spiked with kirsch. I find the trio of flavours play well off each other to create an elegant and well-balanced dessert.

SERVES 8

For the chocolate pots
200g (7oz) dark chocolate (minimum 70% cocoa solids), plus extra (optional), grated
320ml (11fl oz) whole milk
400ml (14fl oz) double cream
65g (2¼oz) caster sugar
1 vanilla pod, split
8 egg yolks

For the kirsch cream
250ml (9fl oz) cold double cream
1–1½ tablespoons sugar
1 scant tablespoon kirsch or other cherry brandy

Sweet Roasted Cherries (page 22), to serve

Preheat the oven to 160°C/325°F/gas mark 3.

Place the chocolate in a large heatproof bowl. Fill a saucepan with water and bring it to the boil. Remove it from the heat and place the bowl of chocolate on top, ensuring it doesn't come into contact with the water. Allow the chocolate to melt gradually. In a separate saucepan, combine the milk, cream and sugar. Scrape the seeds from the vanilla pod, then add both the seeds and pod to the mixture. Place over a medium high heat and bring to a simmer. While the milk is heating, put the egg yolks into a clean bowl, with a towel underneath to secure it. When the milk is hot to touch and the sugar has dissolved, remove from the heat and discard the vanilla pod. Slowly begin to ladle the milk into the eggs, whisking continuously. Once all the milk is added, pour over the chocolate and, switching to a spatula or wooden spoon, slowly mix the chocolate into the milk. Strain the entire mixture through a fine-mesh sieve, then divide evenly between eight ramekins or heatproof ceramic cups.

Place the ramekins into a roasting tin, cover tightly with foil, leaving a corner open to add the water. Place the tray into the oven, then pour enough boiling water into the tray to reach three-quarters of the way up the ramekins. Seal the corner with foil and bake for 15–20 minutes. The custards are done when they begin to set around the edges but have a wobble in the centre. Remove from the hot water and allow them to cool on a wire rack. For the most luscious texture and full expression of flavour, these are best served at room temperature.

To make the kirsch cream, combine the cream and sugar in a bowl and whisk until the metal whisk leaves tracks but just before soft peaks have formed. Add the kirsch, whisk to incorporate and then taste. Adjust the sugar or kirsch to your liking. If this is done in advance, cover and keep chilled.

To serve, toss the roasted cherries in their juices, and place a spoonful on the chocolate pots, followed by a spoonful of softly whipped kirsch cream. Finish with a little drizzle of remaining roasted cherry juice.

Roasted Cherry and Peach Leaf Ice Cream

Cherries are delicious to eat out of hand, but their flavour can be challenging to preserve when cooked. That is why, when a pastry chef once approached me for advice on making cherry ice cream, I shared the following instructions. They are representative of the way I cook – they hone in on the flavours of the fruit, adding other ingredients to underpin those flavours, and ultimately creating something that is clear and deeply flavourful.

SERVES 8–10

600g (1lb 5oz) Sweet
 Roasted Cherries with
 Peach Leaves (page 22)
400g (14oz) Plain Ice
 Cream Base (page 16)
sugar, kirsch and lemon
 juice, to taste
Soft Almond Cookies (page
 141), to serve

Squeeze the vanilla pods, zest and peach leaves to extract any remaining liquid, then discard them. Transfer the pitted cherries, along with the flavourful juices, to a blender. Take a spatula to scrape down the roasting tray, avoiding any burnt areas (as they can make the purée bitter). Begin blending on low speed, gradually increasing to medium and then high, until you achieve a smooth purée. If the purée appears chunky or dry, add a splash of kirsch or ice cream base to loosen the consistency.

Once the cherries are smooth, add the rest of the ice cream base and blend on a low speed until everything is combined. Taste and adjust with sugar, kirsch or lemon. Churn in an ice-cream maker following the manufacturer's instructions, then place into the freezer.

Serving suggestions: Serve with Almond Cake (page 175) or Soft Almond Cookies (page 141). Scoop on top of a Coconut Meringue (page 117) with cream or serve with a grating of dark chocolate and Sugared Rose Petals (page 116).

Goat's Cheese Soufflés with Spring Herb Salad and Roasted Cherries

Spring and early summer is a time for tender leaves and soft herbs. Sweet cicely, tarragon and fennel emerge from their winter slumber, while newly sown salad leaves are ready to harvest just as the summer vegetables have started to germinate. This dish is an expression of that brief moment in time when cherries, soft herbs and fresh goat's cheese are at their prime.

SERVES 6

For the goat's cheese soufflés

65g (1¾oz) unsalted butter, plus extra for the ramekins

25g (¾oz) grated Parmesan cheese, plus extra for the ramekins

3 large eggs

3 tablespoons plain flour

200ml (7fl oz) whole milk

1 sprig of thyme

1 bay leaf

150g (5¼oz) mild fresh goat's cheese

¼ teaspoon cream of tartar

salt and pepper

For the topping

100ml (3½fl oz) double cream

100ml (3½fl oz) crème fraîche

Preheat the oven to 190°C/375°F/Gas Mark 5 and generously butter six 150ml (5fl oz) ramekins. Coat the base and sides of each ramekin with Parmesan cheese and set aside. Separate the egg yolks from the whites, placing the whites into a clean, wide bowl.

In a heavy saucepan, melt the butter, then add the flour and stir with a spatula for 2–3 minutes until the roux is hot and starts to bubble. Gradually pour in a quarter of the milk, stirring continuously to remove any lumps. Slowly add the remaining milk, along with the thyme and bay leaf. Cook until the mixture thickens and coats the back of the spatula. Remove from the heat and discard the herbs, then add the Parmesan cheese, followed by the egg yolks, mixing them in one by one. Crumble the goat's cheese into the mixture and stir until completely incorporated.

Next add the cream of tartar and a pinch of salt into the bowl with the egg whites. Whisk the egg whites until stiff and glossy, then fold one-third of the egg whites into the cheese mixture. Gently fold in the rest.

Divide the soufflé batter among the prepared ramekins and place them in a high-sided roasting tray. Carefully pour enough boiling water into the tray to reach halfway up the sides of the ramekins. Seal the top with foil and place in the preheated oven. Bake for 20–25 minutes until the soufflés have risen and set around the edges, with a slight soft wobble in the centre. Remove from the oven and transfer the ramekins to a wire rack to cool. Once completely cool, the soufflés can be turned out of the ramekins and stored in a sealed container in the refrigerator.

Ingredients and recipe continued overleaf

For the spring herb salad
and roasted cherries

400g (14oz) tender mixed
salad leaves and soft
herbs, washed and dried

2 tablespoons Simple
Vinaigrette (see below)

salt and pepper

1 batch Savoury Roasted
Cherries (page 23)

200g (7oz) Honeyed
Walnuts (page 201)

To serve the soufflés, preheat the oven to 200°C/400°F/gas mark 6. Transfer the soufflés to a ceramic baking dish. In a separate bowl, mix the crème fraîche and cream until smooth, then pour over the soufflés. Bake for 15–20 minutes until slightly puffed and golden brown.

While the soufflés are in the oven, prepare your salad. Place the salad leaves in a wide bowl and drizzle with 1 tablespoon of the vinaigrette. Add a pinch of salt and gently toss the leaves to coat them without bruising. Carefully fold in half the roasted cherries and honeyed walnuts. Taste and adjust with additional vinaigrette, salt or pepper if desired. Transfer the salad to a serving plate and scatter the remaining cherries and walnuts on top.

Simple Vinaigrette

Makes about 200ml (6¾fl oz)

1 small shallot, finely diced

2 tablespoons red wine
vinegar

1 tablespoon lemon juice

1 garlic clove

2 teaspoons Dijon mustard

150ml (5fl oz) extra-virgin
olive oil

salt and pepper

Place the diced shallots into a small bowl with the red wine vinegar, lemon juice and a pinch of salt. Leave the shallots to soften for 10–15 minutes. Pound the garlic in a mortar (or it can be smashed on a cutting board using the side of a knife), then transfer the garlic to a bowl with the mustard and macerated shallots. Whisk everything together, then gradually whisk in the olive oil until emulsified. Adjust with salt and pepper. Store in a glass jar in the refrigerator for up to a week.

Stone Fruit

Cherry Schiacciata

Baking bread often demands a time commitment that many of us struggle to accommodate within a single day. That's why I adore this recipe— I can mix it together in under 30 minutes the first day, then let it prove overnight and bake it the following day.

SERVES 6–8

330g (11½oz) bread flour
220ml (8fl oz) warm water
5g (⅛oz) mild honey
5g (⅛oz) active dried yeast
7g (¼oz) salt
4 teaspoons olive oil, plus extra for greasing and drizzling
450g (1lb) cherries, pitted
1 tablespoon fennel seeds (optional)
flaky salt, to finish (I like Maldon or fleur de sel)

Combine the flour, warm water, honey and yeast in a bowl and mix everything together for 2 minutes. Cover loosely with a tea towel and rest in a warm place for 15 minutes. Add the salt and olive oil and continue to mix for another 2 minutes. Meanwhile, coat a large bowl with oil, then add the dough and cover with a towel. Place into the refrigerator overnight.

The following day, place a baking stone or inverted baking tray on the middle shelf of the oven. Take another baking tray and brush the inside generously with olive oil. Remove the dough from the refrigerator and carefully turn it onto the tray. Drizzle the top with more oil, then use the tips of your fingers to gently stretch the dough to 40cm (16in) long. Cover lightly with a tea towel and leave to prove in a warm place for up to 30 minutes. After proving, the dough should be relaxed and risen slightly.

Preheat the oven to 190°C/375°F/gas mark 5.

While the bread is proving, prepare the cherries. Use a cherry pitter to remove the pits. Alternatively, slice the cherries in half, pull out the pits and place the cherries into a bowl. Lightly pound the fennels seeds (if using) with a mortar and pestle, or crush them with the end of a rolling pin.

Dot the cherries over the schiacciata and scatter the fennel seeds evenly over the dough. Slide the tray onto the baking stone and bake for 20–30 minutes or until golden. Remove the schiacciata from the oven and drizzle with more olive oil and sprinkle with large flakes of salt. Serve warm or room temperature. This is best enjoyed on the day it is made, but any leftovers make a nice morning snack.

VARIATION
Replace the pitted cherries with grapes and swap the fennel seeds for rosemary.

PEACH & NECTARINE PAIRINGS

NUTS AND SEEDS	Almond, hazelnut, pecan, pistachio, sesame
FLOWERS, LEAVES AND HERBS	Rose, lavender, lemon verbena, peach leaf
SPICES	Cardamom, cinnamon, ginger, nutmeg, vanilla
FRUITS	Blackberry, blueberry, cherry, coconut, loganberry, melon, passion fruit, plum, raspberry, whitecurrant
VEGETABLES	Courgette, green bean, green chilli, red pepper, rocket, sweetcorn, tomato
FLOURS	Buckwheat, oat, polenta, rye, semolina, spelt, teff
WINES AND SPIRITS	Champagne, red wine, vin de pêche, white wine, bourbon, brandy, kirsch, rum
DAIRY AND MEAT	Brown butter, buttermilk, burrata, cream, feta, mascarpone, ricotta, soft sheep's milk cheese, young goat's cheese, young pecorino, pork, prosciutto
OTHER FLAVOURS	Caramel, honey, maple syrup, olive oil, rose water, treacle

FAVOURITE COMBINATIONS WITH PEACH & NECTARINE

PEACH • RASPBERRY • VANILLA | PEACH • BOURBON • RYE
PEACH • COURGETTE • BASIL | PEACH • PEACH LEAF • RED WINE
PEACH • TOMATO • SWEETCORN • GREEN CHILLI | PEACH • PROSCIUTTO • BURRATA
NECTARINE • PASSION FRUIT • CREAM | NECTARINE • GREEN BEAN • FETA
NECTARINE • LAVENDER • HONEY | NECTARINE • LEMON VERBENA • CREAM
NECTARINE • ALMOND • BLACKBERRY

Peach and Tomato Salsa

Fresh, zesty, sweet and spicy, this salsa boosts any number of summer dishes. Serve with grilled fish or roast chicken. Spoon over tacos, a bowl of warm black beans or simply eat with a bowl of tortilla crisps. Here the peaches should be sweet and yielding, the tomatoes bursting with juice and acidity, and the coriander tender and fresh.

SERVES 4

3 spring onions, white
   parts only, finely diced
zest and juice of ½ lime
2 medium tomatoes
1 bunch of fresh coriander
1 green chilli, preferably
   serrano or jalapeño, finely
   diced
2 ripe peaches, blanched
   (see page 167)
salt

Place the diced spring onions into a bowl with the lime juice and a pinch of salt. Stir to combine, then leave for 30 minutes to soften the onion.

Meanwhile, slice the tomatoes into small chunks and chop the coriander. Add both to the onions along with the diced chilli. Gently fold it with a wide spoon and set aside to let the flavours develop.

Peel the blanched peach and slice into small chunks. Fold through the salsa and taste. Adjust with salt and lime juice, if necessary.

VARIATIONS
Heat: Add an extra chilli or two for a salsa picante.

Mango: Swap 1 mango, diced, for the peach and add another squeeze of lime juice.

Middle Eastern-style Salad: Swap a red onion for the spring onions. Swap 1 tablespoon of red wine vinegar for the lime zest and juice. Chop 1 cucumber and 1 red pepper, then add to the tomatoes and swap the coriander for basil and parsley. Adjust with salt and pepper and finish with olive oil. Serve with warm pitta.

Stone Fruit

Pizza with Peaches, Stracciatella, Rocket and Prosciutto

In this recipe pizza is dotted with peaches and creamy stracciatella, then baked quick and hot until golden. After it comes out of the oven, it is finished with a generous pile of lightly dressed rocket and paper-thin prosciutto.

SERVES 4–6

½ quantity Schiacciata Dough (page 151), omitting the honey

plain flour, for dusting

olive oil

⅛ red onion, sliced as thinly as possible

pinch of chilli flakes

1 juicy, ripe peach, blanched and peeled (page 167)

80g (2¾oz) stracciatella, burrata or fresh mozzarella

handful of rocket

½ teaspoon red wine vinegar

4–5 slices of prosciutto

shaved Parmesan (optional)

salt and pepper

Make the dough the day before, omitting the honey, and place in the refrigerator overnight. The following day, remove the dough from the refrigerator and place on a clean work surface. Shape it into a ball, lightly dusting with flour if the dough feels sticky. Put it into a bowl, cover it with a tea towel and allow it to rest in a warm spot for 30 minutes. Oil a large baking tray or flour a pizza paddle.

Preheat your oven to 220°C/425°F/gas mark 7 and place a baking stone or inverted tray on the middle shelf of the oven.

When the dough is rested, place on the prepared tray or paddle and stretch until it is about 30cm (12in) diameter. Brush the top with olive oil, then arrange the sliced onion and sprinkle some chilli flakes. Stone and slice the peach into 16 wedges and evenly scatter them over the pizza dough. Top with spoonfuls of stracciatella. Slide the tray onto the baking stone and bake for 10–12 minutes until the edges begin to blister and the cheese is melted and bubbly.

While the pizza is cooking, dress the rocket in the vinegar, along with a pinch of salt and a slick of olive oil. Once the pizza is cooked, remove it from the oven and scatter with dressed rocket, followed by the prosciutto and shavings of Parmesan, if using. Serve the pizza immediately, while still hot.

David 'Mas' Masumoto

Masumoto Family Farm, California, USA, Peaches

Organic peaches grow when nature and human nature work in partnership. Working together, collaborating not competing. Constantly changing and transitioning. Adapt. Adopt. Accept.

Soils are alive and living. My dirt is a sandy loam; it's taken generations to learn how to work with it. We call most weeds 'natural grasses', my father said they are a sign the dirt is alive.

The weather has its own life, you're lucky to predict a few days if not hours. Respect inconsistency, learn to watch and witness. It is a mercy we live with and I make adjustments knowing the weather will not accommodate me. Change lies at the heart of the climate crisis.

There is a legacy of working our 80-acre organic farm. We recall those who worked our 100-year-old grapevines in front of the farmhouse, they planted vines then built our old house – priorities. Our 60-year-old heirloom Suncrest peaches took decades to learn how to

grow. We honour farmworkers who contribute with their sweat.

I work with all my senses while I farm. I listen to the sounds of native bees in early spring. I imagine the pop of a peachblossom opening with first warmth (or is it a crackle, or a soft unfolding?) At harvest, I use all my senses to determine a ripe peach – a golden colour in early morning light, the aroma, the feel of the surface and the slight 'give' my fingers have learned over time to detect. And of course I must taste one. I gasp with the first bite of every year as I lose my yearly peach virginity.

There is satisfaction in sharing the fruits of labour. Imagine others taking a bite, and the flood of memories that accompanies great food. A simple childhood moment with juices dripping down your chin or sharing a dish with others. My favourite dish is the peach galette my wife Marcy makes, peach slices carefully laid in a vision of delight.

We have farmed for generations and there is history buried in this land. My grandparents arrived from Japan as immigrants with dreams to plant roots. They faced discrimination, yet these fields were hungry for strong backs and quick hands. During World War II they were uprooted and imprisoned for years as they looked like the enemy. Yet they endured and found resilience to partner with this dirt we call home. I learned to farm with these ghosts, and the legacy I both carry and contribute to as my children Nikiko and Korio now partner with this ageing old farmer.

This is all part of the flavour of a small, organic family farm in the heart of California. All these elements contribute to the sweet taste of our peaches, nectarines, apricots and raisins, and are ingredients for the stories I write and share. Stories define and drive me to keep working, walking these fields as generations have before and if fortune continues, others beyond my horizon. All in partnership with nature and human nature.

Salad of Nectarines, Green Beans, Almonds and Feta

The appeal of this salad comes from its contrasting flavours and textures. Make this in midsummer, when the nectarines are ripened by the sun and the green beans are still tender. It is best served on a wide plate, rather than piled into a deep bowl.

SERVES 2 FOR LUNCH OR 4 AS A SIDE SALAD

350–400g (12–14oz) trimmed green beans (haricots verts, wax beans or young flat beans are fine)

3–4 tablespoons Simple Vinaigrette (page 148)

60g (2¼oz) whole almonds, toasted until golden and halved lengthways

75g (2½oz) feta, crumbled

2 ripe and fragrant nectarines

fennel blossoms, tender fennel fronds or green anise (optional)

good-quality oil, for drizzling

salt and pepper

Start by cooking the green beans. Bring a saucepan of water to a rolling boil and add a few pinches of salt. Fill a bowl with cold water and set aside. Drop the trimmed green beans into the boiling water and cook for 1–2 minutes until the green beans begin to soften but still have a snap. Later in the season, when the beans are bigger, cook for 3–4 minutes. Transfer with a slotted spoon to the cold water to stop them cooking, then lay on a clean tea towel to dry.

Place the green beans into a bowl and toss with the vinaigrette, add two-thirds of the almonds and half the feta, then gently fold a couple of times to combine, taking care not to smear the feta into the beans. Stone and slice the nectarines into wedges, and gently fold into the salad. Taste for seasoning, adjust if necessary, then transfer to a wide serving plate. Finish with the rest of the feta and almonds, a drizzle of good oil and pepper. Scatter fennel blossoms over the top (if using) and serve.

VARIATIONS
Duck Salad: Add strips of warm duck breast (page 86) to the salad.

Other Fruits: Swap the nectarines for peaches or plums or add slices of ripe sweet figs to the salad.

Other Cheeses: Swap the feta for ricotta salata or a creamy goat's cheese.

Salad of Nectarines, Green Beans, Almonds and Feta

Coconut Rum Cake
with Peaches in Syrup

In the United States, coconut cake is a staple of Southern cuisine which boasts numerous variations. A particularly beloved adaptation incorporates peaches, a fruit that is abundant in the southeast and has a storied legacy in Southern traditions. This cool, creamy version reaches its full potential when allowed to rest overnight in the refrigerator, during which time the sponge cake soaks up the rum and the custard achieves the perfect consistency. This cake is also delicious with Macerated Strawberries (page 100), Any Berry Compote (page 109) or Poached Kumquats (page 65).

SERVES 12

For the coconut cream
400ml (14fl oz) double cream
80g (2¾oz) toasted coconut, plus extra to serve (optional)
70g (2½oz) sugar

For the cake
115g (4oz) grapeseed oil
2 eggs
110ml (3¾fl oz) water
½ teaspoon vanilla extract
215g (7½oz) plain flour
75g (2½oz) coconut flour
½ teaspoon salt
2 teaspoons baking powder
125g (4½oz) caster sugar (first measure)
225g (8oz) egg whites (about 7 eggs)
½ teaspoon cream of tartar
125g (4 ½oz) caster sugar (second measure)

The day before you serve the cake, combine the toasted coconut with the double cream and place it into the fridge to infuse overnight.

On the day you're making the cake preheat the oven to 160°C/325°F/gas mark 3. Take two 9in (22cm) cake tins and brush the sides and bottoms thoroughly with oil, then line the bases with baking parchment and dust the insides with flour.

To make the cake, combine the oil, eggs, water and vanilla in a mixing bowl, whisking until smooth. In another bowl, sift together all the dry ingredients and whisk in the first measure of sugar. Gradually incorporate the wet mixture into the dry ingredients and set aside.

In a separate bowl, whisk the egg whites and cream of tartar until light and frothy. Slowly add the second measure of sugar, whisking until stiff but not dry. Begin by gently folding a third of the egg whites into the cake batter to lighten it, then follow with the remaining egg whites. Ensure everything is combined but be gentle to maintain airiness. Pour the batter into the prepared cake tins and bake for 15–20 minutes, or until lightly coloured and a toothpick inserted into the centre comes out clean. Cool the cakes in their tins on a wire rack, and don't be alarmed if they deflate slightly, this is normal.

While the cakes cool, prepare the coconut filling. Heat the coconut milk, vanilla seeds and salt in a saucepan over a medium heat. In a bowl, whisk the sugar, cornflour and eggs until smooth. When the coconut milk is almost boiling, carefully pour a bout a quarter of it into the egg mixture, whisking constantly, to temper the eggs.

Ingredients and recipe continued overleaf

For the coconut filling

650ml (29fl oz) coconut milk

½ vanilla pod, split and seeds removed

½ teaspoon salt

90g (3oz) sugar

35g (1¼oz) cornflour

2 eggs

20g (¾oz) cold butter, cubed

For the rum soak

2 teaspoons water

2 teaspoons sugar

2 teaspoons lime juice

2 teaspoons dark rum

To serve

1 quantity Peaches in Syrup (see below)

Pour the mixture into the rest of the milk in the pan and continue to cook, whisking constantly, until the mixture begins to boil. Remove from the heat and whisk in the butter cubes, one by one, until emulsified. Pass through a fine-mesh sieve into a clean bowl, then cover and allow to cool in the refrigerator.

For the rum soak, heat the water and sugar in a small saucepan until the sugar dissolves. Add the lime juice and rum and allow the mixture to cool to room temperature.

When you are ready to assemble, remove the cakes from their tins and slice each one in half.Cut two pieces of clingfilm, preferably biodegradable, each measuring approximately 63cm (25in) in length. Line a clean 22cm (9in) cake tin with these pieces of cling film, ensuring that they cover the tin's walls and have plenty of overhang. Place the first layer of cake into the tin, then brush with ¼ of the rum soak and spread one-third of the coconut pudding evenly over the top. Repeat with the other layers, finishing with the final layer of cake and rum soak. Tightly wrap it with the overhanging cling film. Place a plate on top of the cake and add a light weight, such as a jar of jam or a tin of beans, to apply gentle pressure. Refrigerate the cake overnight.

The following day, strain the toasted coconut cream through a fine mesh sieve, add the sugar, and whip to soft peaks. Remove the cake from the refrigerator, unmould from the tin and cover with toasted coconut cream and more toasted coconut if desired. Serve slices of the coconut cake with Peaches in Syrup and glasses of chilled rum.

PEACHES IN SYRUP

400ml (14fl oz) water

300g (10½oz) caster sugar

juice of ¼ lemon

3 juicy, ripe peaches, yielding at the base

Combine the water and sugar in a small saucepan and warm to dissolve the sugar, remove from the heat and cool completely, then stir in the lemon juice. (This can be made in advance and stored in the refrigerator for up to a week.) Blanch the peaches (page 167), then peel, stone and slice into wedges about 2cm (¾in) thick and slip them into the syrup. Cover the top of the peaches with a small piece of baking parchment to keep them submerged and allow to sit for 15 minutes.

Vin de Pêche

This fortified aperitif relies on peach leaves for its flavour. Peach leaves can be difficult to source conventionally, so ask a farmer in your local area, or enquire with a friend who may have a tree in their garden. The leaves should be organic and unsprayed. The best time to harvest peach leaves is in late spring or early summer. As the fruit develops, it will draw energy (and flavour) from the leaves, so it is best to harvest before the fruit has set.

MAKES A GENEROUS 1 LITRE (34FL OZ)

100 young peach leaves, cleaned and patted dry (about 2 handfuls)
750ml (23½fl oz) fruity red wine
300g (10½) caster sugar
150ml (5fl oz) brandy

Place all the ingredients in a non-reactive container, preferably made of glass. Gently stir to dissolve the sugar, then seal and label with the date. As direct sunlight and heat can oxidize wine, it is best to store this in a cool, dark place.

After 2 weeks, give the vin de pêche a stir, then cover and store for another 2 weeks. After a month has passed, strain the peach leaves and transfer to glass bottles. The vin de pêche is now ready to serve.

You may simply enjoy poured over ice or make the Raspberry and Vin de Pêche Granita (page 112) and serve with fresh peaches.

VARIATIONS

White or Rosé Wine: A few years ago, my sister substituted white wine for the red. We drank it on a hot summer's eve after a dinner of grilled fish and yellow tomatoes confit. It was heavenly.

Warm: This may seem sacrilegious to lovers of vin de pêche, but I served this one summer evening on my friend's farm when unexpected rains brought in the wet and the chill. Gently warm the wine on the hob (but do not boil), then drop in a handful of fresh raspberries and ladle into glasses. Kick off your wellies, put up your feet and enjoy.

Honey Lavender Ice Cream with Fresh Peaches

The flavour of lavender has fallen out of fashion over the last few years, which is a shame because when used in moderation, good-quality lavender can be complex and seductive. The mix of floral, herbaceous and earthy aromas give it an alluring charm. The freshest lavender can be found at farmers' markets, or if you choose to grow some at home, seek out a variety suitable for culinary use, such as *Lavandula angustifolia*. Here the ice cream is served with Peaches in Syrup. When peaches make way for figs later in the summer, serve this ice cream with the Fig Galette with Summer Berry Compote (page 181).

SERVES 8–10

400ml (14fl oz) double
  cream
400ml (14fl oz) whole milk
60g (2¼oz) sugar
1 teaspoon salt
120g (4¼oz) egg yolks
  (about 6 eggs)
70g (2½oz) honey, or
  more according to taste
2 teaspoons fresh culinary
  lavender buds

To serve
1 quantity Peaches in Syrup
  (page 162)

Pour the double cream, milk, sugar and salt into a heavy, non-reactive saucepan and place over a medium heat. Take two large bowls and add iced water to the largest bowl, nestling the other bowl inside. Sit a fine-mesh sieve over the top bowl and set it aside somewhere nearby.

Whisk the yolks in a separate bowl, then wrap a towel around the base to stabilize it. Once the milk mixture begins to simmer, gradually add the hot milk to the yolks, whisking constantly as you pour. (If your saucepan is too heavy to hold with one hand, then use a ladle or small cup.) Return the mixture to the pan and reduce to a medium–low heat. Gently cook, stirring constantly until the mixture is thick enough to coat the back of a spoon. Remove the saucepan from the heat and strain the mixture through the fine-mesh sieve into the cold bowl over the ice. Add the honey and lavender and continue to cool the mixture fully.

Once the ice cream base is properly chilled pour into a container and store in the refrigerator.

The following day, strain the base through a sieve to remove the lavender. Taste and adjust to your liking. Churn in an ice-cream maker following the manufacturer's instructions, then place into the freezer until you are ready to serve. Serve with slices of Peaches in Syrup.

Stone Fruit

Honey Lavender Ice Cream with Fresh Peaches

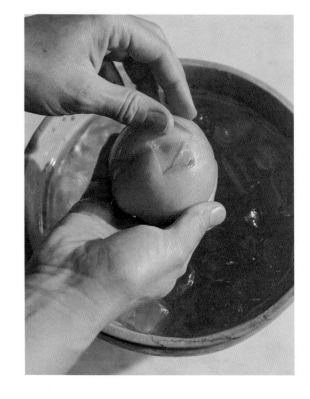

Stone Fruit

HOW TO BLANCH A PEACH

Blanching peaches loosens the furry peel from the flesh, making it easy to remove the skins. You'll want to start with blanched peaches when making a peach purée (page 15), Peach Pizza (page 155) or the Peach and Tomato Salsa (page 153).

Begin by bringing a large pan of water to a rolling boil and have a bowl of iced water close at hand. While the water is heating, score the peaches at the base of the fruit by using a small, sharp knife to slice a shallow X into flesh. This will prevent the peaches from bursting in the hot water. Once the water is at a rolling boil, drop 2–3 peaches into the pan at a time. Crowding too many peaches into the pan will reduce the temperature of the water, prolonging the blanching time, which could potentially cook the fruit. After 10–15 seconds, you will begin to see the skin pull away from the cuts at the base of the fruit. At this point, transfer the peaches to the bowl of iced water to halt the cooking. If you wish to blanch more peaches, wait until the pan returns to a rolling boil, then proceed with the next batch.

Once the peaches are cool enough to touch, pull them out of the water and pat dry with kitchen paper. Starting at the base of the peach, use your fingers to peel back the skin. Discard the skin and transfer the peeled peaches to a plate, or otherwise place into a flat container if you wish to store them in the refrigerator.

If the skins do not release from the peaches, it is possible your peaches are underripe, the water was not hot enough, or they simply weren't blanched for an adequate amount of time. If this happens, use a sharp knife to peel back the skin.

PLUM, DAMSON & GREENGAGE PAIRINGS

NUTS	*Almond, hazelnut, pecan, pistachio, walnut*
FLOWERS, LEAVES AND HERBS	*Fennel blossom, lavender, rose, rose geranium, anise hyssop, bay leaf, coriander, green anise*
SPICES	*Anise, cardamom, fennel seed, ginger,*
FRUITS	*Apple, blackberry, fig, mulberry, nectarine, peach, raspberry*
VEGETABLES	*Beetroot, fennel, green bean, rocket, tomato*
FLOURS	*Polenta, rye*
WINES AND SPIRITS	*Muscat dessert wine, red wine, white wine, brandy, kirsch, pastis*
DAIRY AND MEAT	*Soft triple cream, young goat's cheese, chicken, lamb, pâté, terrine*
OTHER FLAVOURS	*Caramel, honey, olive oil, vanilla*

FAVOURITE COMBINATIONS WITH PLUM, DAMSON & GREENGAGE

PLUM • LAMB • CORIANDER | PLUM • GREEN BEAN • GREEN ANISE
PLUM • PASTIS • PÂTÉ | PLUM • OLIVE OIL • RICOTTA
DAMSON • WALNUT • SHEEP'S MILK CHEESE | DAMSON • VANILLA • CREAM
GREENGAGE • CARDAMOM • PISTACHIO | GREENGAGE • HONEY • BUTTERMILK

Damson Purée

The damson's large stone and low moisture content make it one of the more challenging stone fruits to cook with. Cooking them down can feel like a lot of effort for very little reward. I wish I could offer you a hack, but instead the Damsons Five Ways recipes overleaf will show how to get the most out of your effort. The damsons are first cooked down into a purée, which can then be used for ice cream, sorbet or sauce. The method for puréeing damsons is similar to that for other stone fruits but they require more water and an extended cooking time. The leftover stones and pulp are repurposed into cordial or damson brandy.

As mentioned throughout the recipes, taste and adjust the sugar to your liking. This is especially the case with damsons. The astringency of damsons varies widely, making it difficult to know off the bat how much sugar you will need. Each measurement of sugar below is a conservative one. I wrote it keeping in mind that it is easier to add sugar to a recipe than take it out. Always reserve a small amount of sugar on hand. Taste, adjust and taste again until the dish tastes right to you.

MAKES ABOUT 1–1.2KG (2–2½LB)

1.5kg (3lb 5oz) ripe
   damsons
1½ tablespoons caster
   sugar
300ml (10fl oz) water

Place the damsons into a heavy-based pan with the sugar and water. Cover with a lid and place over a high heat. When the fruit begins to break down, turn down the heat to medium and lightly bash the fruit until it is completely submerged in the liquid. Cover and continue to cook for 10 minutes, checking the pan once or twice to make sure the fruit isn't catching and burning on the bottom.

Meanwhile, place a food mill or wide-holed colander over a large bowl. After 10 minutes, the fruit should have completely collapsed. If your fruit was firm to begin with, this may take a few more minutes. When the fruit is thoroughly broken down, carefully ladle the hot purée into the food mill and pass through. (Alternatively, use a ladle or soft spatula to press the damsons through a large-holed colander.) Set aside the damson stones for another use (see overleaf) and allow the purée to cool. When the purée is cool enough to handle, pour into a blender and blitz until silky smooth.

Damson purée will keep in the fridge for up to 5 days, or in the freezer for up to 6 months.

Damsons 5 Ways

FIRST WAY: DAMSON ICE CREAM

SERVES 8–10

550g (1lb 4oz) Damson
   Purée (page 169)
500ml (18fl oz) Plain Ice
   Cream Base (page 16)
180g (6oz) caster sugar,
   plus extra to taste
squeeze of lemon juice

Combine all the ingredients together in a blender and adjust the sweetness if necessary. Churn in an ice-cream maker following the manufacturer's instructions, then place into the freezer until you are ready to serve.

SECOND WAY: DAMSON SORBET

SERVES 8–10

900g (2lb) Damson Purée
   (page 169)
100ml (3½fl oz) water
400g (14oz) caster sugar
squeeze of lemon juice

Combine all the ingredients together and adjust the sweetness if necessary. Churn in an ice-cream maker following the manufacturer's instructions, then place into the freezer until you are ready to serve.

THIRD WAY: DAMSON SAUCE

SERVES 8–10

500g (1lb 2oz) Damson
    Purée (page 169)
180g (6oz) sugar
squeeze of lemon juice

Combine all the ingredients in a saucepan and cook over a medium heat until the sauce looks glossy and smooth. If the damson sauce seems a bit thick, then stir in 50ml (1¾fl oz) of water or enough to give the desired consistency. For an even smoother texture, pass through a fine-mesh sieve. Serve with Frozen Yoghurt-Honey Parfait (page 122) and Honeyed Walnuts (page 201), or Almond Cake (page 175) and Fior di Latte (page 138).

FOURTH WAY: DAMSON CORDIAL

MAKES ABOUT 750ML (25FL OZ)

500g (1lb 2oz) damson
    skins and stones (page
    169)
100g (3½oz) damsons,
    roughly chopped
250–300g (7oz–10½oz)
    sugar
500ml (18fl oz) water

Place the damson skins, stones and damsons into a heavy-based pan and add just enough cold water to cover. Place over a medium–high heat and bring to the boil. Reduce the heat slightly and simmer for 20 minutes. Strain the damsons and measure the liquid. Return the liquid to the pan and for every 100ml (3½fl oz) of liquid, add 200g (7oz) of sugar. Bring to the boil, then reduce the heat and simmer for a further 10 minutes. Allow to cool then decant into bottles and store in the fridge. Serve with sparkling water and wedges of lemon.

FIFTH WAY: DAMSON BRANDY

MAKES ABOUT 1 LITRE (34FL OZ)

750g (1lb 10oz) damson
    skin and stones (page
    169)
100g (3½oz) damsons,
    roughly chopped
750ml (26fl oz) brandy
200g (7oz) sugar

Combine all the ingredients in a clean, sterilized jar. Stir to dissolve the sugar, then seal tightly and leave in a cool, dark place. Flip the jar once a week for the first month (alternatively, give the jar a little shake if it won't stand upside down). Store for another month, then strain and decant into bottles. The brandy will improve with age and keep for up to a year.

Stone Fruit

Almond Cake with Greengages and Fennel Cream

Those fortunate enough to have access to flowering fennel plants may discover their blooms are the most fragrant in late summer when greengages appear on the market. Don't worry if fennel blossom is not available, this cake is also excellent with lightly toasted fennel seed.

SERVES 8–10

For the fennel cream
250ml (9fl oz) double
  cream
4–5 heads of fennel
  blossom (or 1 teaspoon
  lightly toasted fennel
  seed)
1–2 tablespoons sugar

For the almond cake
115g (4oz) almond flour
80g (2¾oz) icing sugar, plus
  extra for dusting
220g (8oz) caster sugar
195g (7oz) unsalted butter
  at room temperature,
  plus extra for greasing
5 large eggs
1 teaspoon vanilla extract
2 tsp almond liqueur
140g (5oz) plain flour
1¾ tsp baking powder
½ tsp salt

For the greengages
500g (1lb 2oz) greengages,
  halved and stoned
40g (1½oz) honey
60g (2¼oz) sugar
2 strips of lemon zest

The day before you bake the cake, make the fennel cream. Place the double cream into a container. Snip the fennel blossoms just below the heads and add to the cream. (Alternatively, crush the toasted fennel seed and add to the cream.) Place into the refrigerator overnight.

To make the cake, preheat the oven to 160°C/325°F/gas mark 3. Grease a 23cm (9in) cake tin with butter and dust it with flour. Line the bottom of the pan with a round of baking parchment. In the bowl of a food processor, grind the almond flour and both sugars until properly mixed. Cube the butter and scatter over the top, then process until the batter is very smooth and fluffy. Add the eggs, one at a time, processing a bit before the next addition. (You may need to remove the lid and scrape the sides to make sure the eggs are fully incorporated.) Add the vanilla and almond liqueur.

Sift together the plain flour, baking powder and salt, then add half the dry ingredients to the processor. Pulse the machine a few times, then add the rest, pulsing until the dry ingredients are just barely incorporated. Scrape down the sides and the blade, then pulse once more. Scrape the batter into the prepared tin and bake the cake for 30 minutes. Rotate the cake 180 degrees, then bake for another 15 minutes or until a skewer inserted into the centre comes out clean. Remove from the oven and place the tin on a wire rack to cool.

To poach the greengages, combine the honey, sugar, lemon zest and 200ml (7fl oz) of water in a saucepan. Over a low heat, gently dissolve the sugar before adding the greengages. Simmer the fruit for 7–10 minutes before removing with a slotted spoon.

To serve, remove the fennel cream from the refrigerator and strain into a bowl. Add the sugar and whip to soft peaks. Dust the top of the cake with icing sugar, then serve slices with spoonfuls of the poached greengages and generous dollops of fennel blossom cream.

North African Lamb with Plums

Plums add brightness and a touch of sweetness to this sticky, spice-scented lamb. Serve with steamed couscous or rice and something green like slow-cooked chard.

SERVES 6–8

1.2–1.5kg (2lb 10oz–3lb 5oz) lamb shoulder, on the bone, excess fat trimmed
2 teaspoons cumin seeds
2 teaspoons coriander seeds
2 garlic cloves
1 fresh red chilli, deseeded and finely chopped
3cm (1¼in) piece of ginger, finely chopped
olive oil
2 medium onions, sliced
10 medium plums
1 cinnamon stick
salt and pepper

For the chermoula
1cm (½in) piece of ginger, peeled and diced
1 fresh red chilli, deseeded and finely chopped
1 garlic clove
½ teaspoon toasted cumin seeds
2 slices Lemon Confit in Oil (see page 41) finely chopped, or the zest of 1 lemon
juice of ½ lemon
25g (1oz) flat-leaf parsley
50g (1¾oz) fresh coriander

Lightly score the top of the lamb shoulder, then season with salt and pepper. Toast the cumin and coriander seeds until fragrant, then place them in a mortar with the garlic and pound into a paste. Add the red chilli, ginger and a tablespoon or two of olive oil and mix together. Rub the marinade over the lamb shoulder, then cover and refrigerate overnight. Remove from the refrigerator 2 hours before cooking and allow it to come to room temperature.

Preheat the oven to 160°C/325°F/gas mark 3.

Scatter the onions over the base of a roasting tray. Slice four of the plums, removing the stones, then add them to the tray with the cinnamon. Place the lamb on top, skin side up, and add 400ml (14fl oz) of water. Cover loosely with a piece of foil and roast for 2 hours. Flip the lamb and cook, covered for another 2 hours. Remove the foil and turn the lamb once more, so the skin side is facing up. Add a splash of more water if the tray looks dry, then place it back into the oven, uncovered, and increase the temperature to 180°C/350°F/gas mark 4. Continue to cook for 1–1½ hours, basting every 30 minutes or so, until the skin is crisp and the meat is falling from the bone. Remove from the oven, transfer the lamb to a board and allow it to rest in a warm place, loosely covered, for at least 30 minutes.

Increase the temperature to 220°C/425°F/gas mark 7 and halve and stone the remaining six plums. Place them into a ceramic casserole. Strain the juices from the roasting tray, then pour enough juice over the plums to come up one-third of the way. Reserve the leftover juices. Roast in the oven for 10–15 minutes until plums are soft and slightly caramelized around the edges.

For the chermoula, place the ginger, red chilli, garlic, cumin and a pinch of salt in a mortar and pound into a paste. Transfer to a bowl and add the confit lemon and lemon juice. Finely chop the parsley and coriander, then fold into the other ingredients and add the oil. Taste and adjust the seasoning if necessary.

To serve, carve the lamb into portions and arrange on a platter. Top with roasted plums, drizzle over any remaining juices, and accompany with a bowl of chermoula.

North African Scented Lamb with Plums

OTHER ORCHARD & VINE FRUIT

FIG, GRAPE, PERSIMMON

Figs flourish in regions with long summers and hot climates. They need to ripen on the tree but, once ripe, their shelf life is short. This makes truly delicious figs difficult to source in cooler climates. Nevertheless, it is not impossible. Look for figs that are soft and beginning to wrinkle around the stem. While small tears in the skin are typical in ripe figs, avoid figs which show signs of mould or rot. Grapes should appear plump and be grouped in large, healthy clusters. When selecting grapes for cooking, opt for those identified by their variety as they often possess a more interesting flavour. If you live near a wine region, consider exploring local markets around harvest time for wine grape varieties. Check the stems for signs of freshness, and lastly, taste the grapes for flavour. Originating in Indochina, persimmons have become especially cherished in Japan as the national fruit. They fall into two main categories: astringent and non-astringent. The term 'astringent' refers to the high levels of tannins that gradually mellow as the fruit ripens. Non-astringent varieties, such as Fuyu, have lower tannins and can be enjoyed best when firm. Astringent varieties include Kaki and Hachiya. When purchasing persimmons, it's important to be able to differentiate between astringent and non-astringent varieties.

FIG PAIRINGS

NUTS AND SEEDS	*Almond, hazelnut, pine nut, pistachio, walnut, sesame*
FLOWERS, LEAVES AND HERBS	*Fennel blossom, rose petal, bay leaf, fig leaf, fennel frond, thyme*
SPICES	*Aniseed, cardamom, black pepper, fennel seed, five spice, star anise, vanilla*
FRUITS	*Blackberry, coconut, grape, mulberry, raspberry*
VEGETABLES	*Beetroot, escarole, fennel, frisée, green bean, radicchio, rocket*
FLOURS	*Buckwheat, einkorn, rye, spelt, teff*
WINES AND SPIRITS	*Marsala, muscat dessert wine, port, red wine, sherry, pastis*
DAIRY, MEAT AND FISH	*Crème fraîche, blue cheese, goat's cheese, goat's milk, Gruyère, mascarpone, pecorino, soft cow's milk cheese, chicken, duck, pork, prosciutto, quail, anchovy*
OTHER FLAVOURS	*Honey, balsamic vinegar, vincotto*

FAVOURITE COMBINATIONS WITH FIG

MULBERRY • ANISEED | QUAIL • FRISÉE | GRAPE • RICOTTA • HAZELNUT
BLUE CHEESE • HONEY • WALNUT | ALMOND • ANCHOVY
ALMOND • MUSCAT | HONEY • LAVENDER | SPELT • RASPBERRY
FENNEL • RYE | FIG LEAF • COCONUT | GOAT'S CHEESE • BEETROOT • VINCOTTO
PORK • GREEN BEAN | FIG LEAF • GOAT'S CHEESE

Other Orchard & Vine Fruit

Fig Galette with Summer Berry Compote

Galettes have a rustic, free-form nature, which makes them an easier and less-stressful alternative to pies and tarts. Once you get a feel for handling the dough, galettes can be made throughout the year using a wide variety of fruits. Not only is this fig galette beautiful and delicious, it is also an excellent introduction to the art of galette-making since it is easy to assemble and bakes well.

SERVES 8–10

For the rough puff pastry
450g (1lb) plain flour, plus extra for dusting
1½ tablespoons sugar
½ teaspoon salt
325g (11½oz) cold unsalted butter
170–200ml (6–7fl oz) ice-cold water

For the frangipane
100g (3½oz) ground almonds (preferably freshly ground from whole nuts, but almond flour is fine too)
10g (¼oz) lightly toasted noyau (page 137, optional)
100g (3½oz) icing sugar
15g (¼oz) plain flour
100g (3½oz) unsalted butter, cubed and then left at room temperature
1 egg
pinch of salt
1 teaspoon vanilla extract (optional)
1 teaspoon bitter almond liqueur (optional)

For the pastry, place the flour, sugar and salt into a mixing bowl and whisk together. Cut the butter into 2cm (¾in) cubes and leave on a plate until it comes to room temperature. You'll know it's ready when you can press it with your finger and it yields slightly. If the butter cracks, then it's too cold and you should continue to temper. If it yields, but looks shiny from the fat, it is too warm and should be placed back into the refrigerator for 5 minutes or so.

When the butter is ready, add it to the mixing bowl and toss to coat in flour. With clean, dry hands, begin to smash the butter pieces with the palm of your hand. If at any point the butter begins to feel greasy, it is too warm. Simply stop what you are doing and transfer the bowl to the refrigerator. Wait 10 minutes, then continue to flatten the butter until no cubes remain. Measure half the water and sprinkle over the flour. Mix the water into the dough, taking care not to work the butter too much. Do this by creating a claw with your hands and mixing in a circular motion, while lifting the drier bits from the bottom of the bowl. Add the remaining water and continue to mix until everything is shaggy and evenly moistened. Lift the dough onto a clean work surface and if any dry bits remain, add a few more drops of ice-cold water to bring them together, then add to the dough. Begin to bring the dough together with a rolling pin. Roll it once (it's fine if it doesn't hold together), then fold the shaggy dough and roll it twice more. Press the rest of the dough together, then divide and form into two discs. Wrap them in baking parchment, then smooth out the edges and flatten into an even layer. Store in the refrigerator overnight to relax the glutens and allow the dough to properly hydrate. The second dough can be frozen for up to 6 months.

The following day, unwrap the pastry and lightly dust your work surface with flour Place the dough in the centre of your work surface and lightly flour. Starting from the centre, begin to roll the dough outward. Give the dough a quarter turn and continue to roll, turning and rolling into an even circle that is about 25cm (10cm) in diameter. If the dough is hard to roll, leave it on the surface for 5 minutes to soften. If the dough feels too soft or begins to stick, transfer it to a piece of parchment and place it back into the refrigerator. When the dough is rolled to the desired size, transfer to a large piece of parchment and chill until you are ready to use it.

Ingredients and recipe continued overleaf

Other Orchard & Vine Fruit

1.2kg (2lb 10oz) ripe,
   jammy figs

caster sugar

cornflour

melted butter, for brushing

demerara sugar, for
   sprinkling

Mixed Berry Compote,
   made using summer
   berries (page 109)

crème fraîche, Honey
   Lavender Ice Cream (page
   164) or Fennel Cream
   (page 175), to serve

For the frangipane, combine the ground almonds, noyau (if using), icing sugar and flour in a food processor. Pulse a few times to mix everything together. With the motor running, drop in the cubes of softened butter. Stop the machine and scrape the sides, then turn the motor on and add the egg, salt and the vanilla extract and/or liqueur, if using. Scrape down the sides of the processor and pulse a few more times. Transfer the frangipane to a container. If you are using immediately, leave at room temperature, otherwise store in the refrigerator. You will have leftover frangipane, but it will keep in the refrigerator for up to 1 week, or in the freezer for up to 6 months.

To assemble the galette, trim the hard knobbly ends of the figs without removing the whole tip. If the figs are quite small, slice in half, otherwise slice into quarters and set aside. You will have more figs than you need; the extras will be used to make the glaze.

Spread 30g (1oz) of frangipane over the base of the chilled pastry. Create a perimeter with the figs, leaving a 4cm (1½in) border at the edge of the dough. Lay the figs one by one at a 45-degree angle, with the sides of each fig lightly touching each other. Continue to lay the figs in a circular pattern, using the larger slices for the outside circles and saving the smaller sizes for the inner circles. Fold and pinch the edges of the dough into a pleat and chill the galette for 1 hour.

Meanwhile, place the remaining figs into a saucepan and fill with water until all the figs are comfortably submerged. Lightly bash the fruit and bring to the boil, then turn down the heat and simmer for 30 minutes. Strain through a fine-mesh sieve, and gently push down on the fruit with the back of a spoon or ladle. Once you have extracted as much liquid as possible, measure the liquid and for every 200ml (7fl oz), add 1 tablespoon of sugar and ¼ teaspoon of cornflour. Return the liquid to the pan with the sugar and cornflour and cook until thick and glossy. Remove from the heat and cool to room temperature.

Preheat the oven to 220°C/425°F/gas mark 7 and place an inverted baking tray on the middle shelf of the oven.

Slide the galette, on the parchment, onto another baking tray, brush the edges with melted butter and scatter the edges liberally with demerara sugar. Use your thumb or a pastry brush to scrape away any butter or sugar that may have fallen onto the parchment. Put the tray into the oven and cook for 20 minutes. Once the figs begin to cook, remove the galette and sprinkle 1 tablespoon of sugar evenly over the fruit. Place it back into the oven and continue to cook for 20–30 minutes until the pastry is a rich golden brown, the fruit looks jammy and the tips of the figs are beginning to colour. Remove from the oven and onto a wire rack, very carefully pull out the parchment and brush the fruit with a light coat of fig glaze and allow it to cool. Just before serving, use a fork to lift the berries out of the berry compote and dot around the figs. Serve slices of the tart with the sauce from the compote and spoonfuls of crème frâiche, Fennel Cream or Honey Lavender Ice Cream.

Fig Galette with Summer Berry Compote

Fig Anchoïade

Anchoïade on toast is an aperitif's best friend. The sweet addition of figs puts it firmly into summer and tempers the intensity of the anchovies. In addition to aperitif hour, these toasts can be served next to a green salad with sweet peppers or green beans, or as a condiment to grilled lamb.

MAKES 450G (1LB)

2 garlic cloves
5 anchovies
1 sprig of thyme
3 large ripe figs, or 5
  smaller ones
1 tablespoon red wine
  vinegar
50g (1¾oz) blanched
  almonds
4 tablespoons good-quality
  olive oil, plus extra to
  serve
thin slices of country-style
  bread, toasted

Preheat the oven to 170°C/340°F/gas mark 3½.

Toast the almonds for 15–20 minutes until lightly golden, then remove them from the oven to cool.

Place the garlic and anchovies into a large mortar, strip the thyme leaves from the stalk and add them to the anchovies. Pound into a paste until the garlic disappears. Trim and roughly chop the figs, then add them to the anchovy paste along with the vinegar. Pound in the almonds until finely broken. Finally, drizzle in the olive oil. Transfer to a bowl and taste for seasoning. Add more salt or oil if necessary.

Lightly drizzle the olive oil over the toast, spread some of the anchoïade on top and serve. The anchoïade will keep in the refrigerator for 2 days. Bring to room temperature before serving.

Fig Anchoïade

Other Orchard & Vine Fruit

Fig, Fennel Seed and Walnut Bread

This loaf resembles a fruit cake in that it is essentially dried figs and walnuts, bound together by a thin layer of lightly sweetened batter. It is firm, moist and lasts for several days. Serve it for breakfast or with a slice of cheese.

MAKES 1 x 450G (1LB) LOAF

340g (11¾oz) walnuts
butter, for greasing
600g (1lb 5oz) good-quality
  dried figs
1½ tablespoons fennel
  seeds
140g (5oz) muscovado
  sugar
3 eggs
65g (2¼oz) wholemeal
  flour, plus extra for
  dusting
65g (2¼oz) dark rye flour
½ teaspoon baking powder
¼ teaspoon salt

Preheat the oven to 170°C/340°F/gas mark 3½.

Toast the walnuts for 15–20 minutes until lightly golden, then remove them from the oven, place on a tea towel and gently rub to remove the skins.

Prepare a 450g (1lb) loaf tin by greasing with butter and dusting with flour, then line the bottom with baking parchment. Remove the stems from the figs and slice into thirds. Place them into a bowl with the walnuts.

Lightly toast the fennel seeds in a hot pan until fragrant, then crush using a mortar and pestle. Alternatively, use the end of a rolling pin.

In another bowl, whisk the crushed fennel with the sugar and eggs. Add the two flours, baking powder and salt and mix until incorporated, taking care that no clumps form. Gently fold in the figs and walnuts.

Pour into the prepared tin, scraping in the last bit of batter and seeds and press the batter well into the tin. It may look like too much batter, but it will fit. Continue to press the fruit down and smooth out the top. Bake for 1½–2 hours until a toothpick inserted into the centre comes out clean. If it gets too dark along the way, lightly cover with foil. Leave to cool in its tin on a wire rack. Then wrap in an airtight container and store at room temperature for up to 5 days.

Other Orchard & Vine Fruit

COOKING WITH AROMATIC LEAVES AND FLOWERS

Aromatic leaves and flowers compliment a wide variety of fruits. To capture these flavours, I infuse them into cream, milk or syrup. However, cooking with these ingredients requires care. If exposed to prolonged heat, the bitterness is extracted from leaves and flowers, masking their best flavours. Hence, I prefer either a long cold steep or a brief hot steep, as detailed below. When at all possible, try to use leaves, herbs or flowers that are unsprayed, organic and freshly cut. For ideas on growing your own see Cooking Starts in the Garden (page 223).

Cold steep: Liquid is poured over leaves or flowers and left to infuse in the refrigerator overnight. I use this method for creams meant to be served lightly whipped and sweetened alongside cake or poached fruit, as well as flavoured syrups to be poured over cakes or used in cordials. Infuse cream with lemon verbena to whip and serve with Peaches in Syrup (page 162) or steep milk with roses for fior di latte ice cream (page 138). Leave two heads of elderflower in buttermilk overnight, then strain and use in the Lemon and Buttermilk Dressing (page 44) but omit the additional herbs. When combining these flavours with fruit ensure they complement each other, and keep the aromatic notes in the background.

Hot steep: In this method, leaves and flowers are plunged into a hot liquid or folded through roasted fruit and returned to the oven for the last few minutes of cooking. The heat draws out the flavour, but the leaves or flowers are removed before any bitter or astringent compounds are extracted. It is also the best method for steeping herbs like mint that easily oxidize. This approach is perfect for jams, roasted fruit or ice creams. To flavour milk, cream or syrup, bring the liquid to the boil, then add a small handful of leaves or flowers and swirl them around while maintaining a consistent boil. After a short swirl, remove the herbs to a separate container. Restraint is required to extract the delicate notes with none of the bitterness. Wait until the mixture reaches the boil once again, then continue with another handful of leaves, tasting as you go until you have the desired flavour.

Time in hot steep	Leaves and flowers
< 15 seconds	Peach leaves, mint leaves, plum blossoms, lavender
< 1 minute	Rose petals, lemon verbena, scented geraniums, blackcurrant leaves, elderflower, fennel blossoms
2–3 minutes	Fig leaves, noyau, bay leaf

GRAPE PAIRINGS

NUTS	*Almond, fresh walnut, hazelnut, peanut*
LEAVES AND HERBS	*Bay leaf, fig leaf, rosemary, thyme*
SPICES	*Anise, fennel seed, mustard seed*
FRUIT	*Apple, blackberry, fig, orange, pear, plum*
VEGETABLES	*Beetroot, endive, fennel, radicchio, rocket, salad leaf, shallot*
FLOURS	*Polenta, rye, semolina, spelt*
WINES AND SPIRITS	*Dessert wine, marsala, red wine, rosé wine, sherry, white wine, brandy, cognac*
DAIRY AND MEAT	*Blue cheese, chocolate, crème fraîche, goat's cheese, Parmesan, chicken, duck, pork, quail*
OTHER FLAVOURS	*Honey, olive oil, red wine vinegar*

FAVOURITE COMBINATIONS WITH GRAPE

PEANUT • SPELT | FIG • BLUE CHEESE | CHOCOLATE • HAZELNUT | QUAIL • RADICCHIO
CHICKEN • MARSALA | OLIVE OIL • BAY LEAF | FENNEL SEED • RICOTTA | BLACKBERRY • CREAM
ROSEMARY • SHALLOT | PORK • MUSTARD SEED

Other Orchard & Vine Fruit

Roasted Grapes Two Ways

Roasted grapes can be spooned over a slice of ricotta or served with grilled duck. Fold through roasted figs and serve with cake or a crème caramel. Similar to blueberries, grapes require a brief stint in a hot oven; this allows their juices to concentrate and the flesh to soften before the fruit breaks down.

SERVES 6

SAVOURY

500g (1lb 2oz) dark grapes, such as black Muscat, Fragolina, Concord, or similar

a small handful of herbs, such as bay leaf, thyme or rosemary

1 teaspoon caster sugar (optional)

1 tablespoon red wine vinegar

1 tablespoon good-quality olive oil

Preheat the oven to 220°C/425°F/gas mark 7.

Place the grapes on a roasting tray big enough for them to lay comfortably in an even layer. Scatter the herbs over the grapes and sprinkle with 2 tablespoons of water. Roast the grapes for 2–3 minutes until the juice at the edges of the tray begin to sizzle. Give the grapes a little shake to make sure they are not catching on the bottom of the tray, then scatter the sugar evenly over the top. Give the tray another shake to distribute the sugar, then return to the oven for another 4–6 minutes. The grapes are done when the skins begin to darken and a few have started to burst. Remove from the oven while the majority of the grapes remain whole.

Immediately splash the grapes with the vinegar and drizzle the oil on top. Shake the tray to coat the grapes then transfer the tray to a wire rack and allow to cool. These are best served the day they are made, but they will keep for up to 3 days in the refrigerator.

SWEET

500g (1lb 2oz) dark grapes, such as black Muscat, Fragolina, Concord, or similar

1½ tablespoons caster sugar

2 teaspoons red wine vinegar

1 tablespoon Vin Santo, sweet marsala, Banyuls or other dessert wine (optional)

Preheat the oven to 220°C/425°F/gas mark 7.

Place the grapes onto a roasting tray big enough for them to lay comfortably in an even layer and sprinkle with 2 tablespoons of water. Roast the grapes for 2–3 minutes until the juices at the edges of the tray begin to sizzle. Give the grapes a little shake to make sure they are not catching on the bottom of the tray, then scatter the sugar evenly over the top. Shuffle the tray to distribute the sugar, then return to the oven for another 4–6 minutes. The grapes are done when the skins begin to darken and a few have started to burst. Remove from the oven while the majority of the grapes remain whole.

Immediately splash the grapes with the vinegar and sweet wine, if using. Shake the tray to coat the grapes and then transfer the tray to a wire rack and allow to cool. These are best served the day they are made, but they will keep for up to 3 days in the refrigerator.

Chocolate Tart with Marsala Sabayon and Toasted Hazelnuts

Marsala is a fortified wine from Sicily that was once popular among chefs and wine enthusiasts alike. However, excessive production cheapened its quality over time, leading to a decline in its reputation. Fortunately, a select few winemakers continue to produce marsala in its authentic form, capturing its deep and mellow character with notes of muscovado and sun-dried fruit. If you haven't any already, now may be the time to add a bottle to your pantry. In this recipe, sweet marsala is used in a sabayon (or *zabaglione* in Italian). Both creamy and light, this boozy custard is traditionally served with summer fruits. But I have opted to serve it with a chocolate tart and toasted hazelnuts.

SERVES 10–12

For the chocolate tart shell
150g (5½oz) unsalted butter, softened, plus extra for greasing
90g (3¼oz) icing sugar, sifted
1 egg
½ teaspoon salt
200g (7oz) plain flour
50g (1¾oz) cocoa powder

For the chocolate filling
530g (1lb 3oz) good-quality chocolate (70% cocoa solids), broken into pieces
3 egg yolks
200ml (7fl oz) double cream
270ml (9½fl oz) whole milk
1 teaspoon salt

For the chocolate dough, butter the bottom and sides of a 25cm (10in) fluted tart tin, and line the base with baking parchment. Place the butter and icing sugar into a mixing bowl and beat until smooth. Add the egg and salt and continue beating until the egg is absorbed.

Sift in the flour and cocoa powder and mix until everything comes together. The dough may feel dry at this stage, but the crust will have a nicer texture when the dough is cooked.

Using your hands, press the dough as evenly as possible into the prepared tart tin. Place a piece of baking parchment over the dough and use the back of a measuring cup (a small glass will also do) to gently press the dough into a smooth even layer. Press the dough up the sides of the tart tin, then trim the excess dough, reserving it for patching up any cracks that may form during baking. Place in the refrigerator until firm.

Preheat the oven to 160°C/325°F/gas mark 3.

Prick the bottom of the tart using a fork, then place it into the oven. After 7 minutes, you may notice the sides of the tart shell beginning to slouch. Gently press a flat-bottomed measuring cup around the edges where the dough has shrunk and encourage it back up the side of the tart tin. Continue to bake for about 20 minutes until the tart shell is cooked all the way through. Remove from the oven and cool on a wire rack.

Ingredients and recipe continued overleaf

Chocolate Tart with Marsala Sabayon and Toasted Hazelnuts

190ml (6½fl oz) double
cream
7 egg yolks
80g (2¾oz) sugar
150ml (5oz) sweet marsala

150g (5½oz) hazelnuts,
lightly toasted and
coarsely chopped, to
serve

For the chocolate filling, prepare two large heatproof bowls – add the chocolate to one and the egg yolks to the other. Fill a saucepan with water and bring it to the boil. Remove it from the heat and place the bowl of chocolate on top, ensuring it doesn't come into contact with the water. Allow the chocolate to melt gradually. Meanwhile, in a separate heavy-based saucepan, combine the double cream, milk and salt. Place it over medium heat. Put your bowl of egg yolks nearby, with a towel underneath to secure it. When the milk mixture begins to simmer, take it off the heat and slowly ladle it into the yolks, stirring constantly with a whisk. Once you have incorporated all the milk into the yolks, return the mixture to the saucepan and place it over a low heat. Stir constantly until the custard thickens slightly and coats the back of a spoon.

Strain through a fine-mesh sieve into the chocolate and let it sit over the hot water for 1 minute. Remove from heat and wipe the water from underneath the bowl. Place a clean, dry spatula into the centre of the chocolate and, using small circular motions, begin to emulsify the chocolate. Once the mixture begins to look glossy, continue to bring in more chocolate and custard, all the while using small circular motions to emulsify the chocolate. Gentle stirring will prevent unwanted air bubbles. If the mixture begins to split, your chocolate may be too hot. However, a small splash of cold milk stirred into the chocolate should bring it back to its glossy texture. Scrape the sides and base of the bowl with spatula every so often. Once the chocolate is properly emulsified, pour into the prepared tart shell and shimmy the tart back and forth to evenly spread the filling. Place in a cool part of the kitchen for 2–3 hours until the filling is set.

For the marsala sabayon, take a small mixing bowl and whip the double cream until the whisk leaves tracks in the cream, stopping before soft peaks form. Chill the whipped cream in the refrigerator until needed. Prepare a large bowl with ice-cold water, filling it about one-third of the way up then set aside. Bring a pan of water to the boil and place the egg yolks into another large heatproof bowl. Sit this on top of the pan of boiling water. Whisk the yolks until they are warm to the touch, then add the sugar and whisk vigorously until the yolks turn pale and thick. Add the marsala and continue whisking until the custard is doubled in size. Notice how the sabayon changes; the bubbles will become smaller and the whisk will leave trails as the mixture thickens and becomes glossy. Remove from the heat and place over the bowl of ice-cold water. Continue whisking until completely chilled. Remove the cream from the refrigerator and whisk to soft peaks. Fold one-third of the sabayon into the cream, then fold in the rest. Store in the refrigerator for up to 4 hours until you are ready to use.

Serve slices of the tart with generous spoonfuls of chilled sabayon and a scattering of toasted hazelnuts.

Eiswein Jelly

One of my first memories after moving to London was tasting an Austrian Eiswein jelly at a charming wine bar near Shoreditch. Eiswein, literally meaning ice wine, is a wine made from grapes that freeze on the vine over winter, concentrating the sugars to make this delectable sweet wine. I was impressed with the clean concentrated sweetness of the grapes and the pure flavour of wine. My version here is set with gelatine and is meant to be served slightly chilled. It's a gratifying addition to any cheese plate. But I think I like it best when sliced into cubes, shining like little jewels in a bowl of frosty fruit sorbet.

SERVES 6

125ml (4fl oz) water
30g (1oz) caster sugar
8g (¼oz) gelatine leaves
95ml (3¼fl oz) sparkling
    wine, such as prosecco
    or cava
280ml (9½fl oz) Eiswein

Gently heat the water and sugar in a small heavy-based saucepan until the sugar dissolves, being careful not to let it boil. Meanwhile, bloom the gelatine in a bowl of ice-cold water. Once the sugar has dissolved, remove the pan from the heat and stir in the softened gelatine. Slowly add the sparkling wine, while stirring to disperse the gelatine, then follow with the Eiswein. Strain through a fine-mesh sieve (in case there are any lumps of undissolved gelatine) into a container, or straight into the serving bowl and place, uncovered, in the refrigerator for 1 hour. At this point the jelly should be cool and starting to set, but still loose. Cover the jelly and place it back into the refrigerator. Continue to let it set for 4–5 hours or overnight.

VARIATIONS
Champagne Jelly: Replace the Eiswein and sparkling wine with 375ml (12fl oz) of champagne and increase the sugar to 40g (1¼oz).

Rosé Jelly: Replace the Eiswein and sparkling wine with 375ml (12fl oz) of fruity rosé and increase the sugar to 40g (1¼oz).

Quail with Charred Radicchio and Grapes

The flavours of charred radicchio and thyme bring warmth to this very autumnal dish. Ask your butcher to spatchcock the birds, which ensures they cook quickly and more evenly. Quail can be swapped for chicken legs, although you will need to increase the cooking time slightly.

SERVES 4

For the quails

4 quails, spatchcocked
1 tablespoon Muscat de Beaumes de Venise
50g (1¾oz) butter, softened
1 sprig of thyme
salt and pepper

For the radicchio

1 medium head of radicchio
olive oil
pinch of salt
300g (10½oz) dark grapes, such as black Muscat, Fragolina, Concord, or similar, on the stem
1 bay leaf
1 tablespoon Muscat de Beaumes de Venise
1 tablespoon balsamic vinegar

Season the quails lightly with salt and pepper. Mix the Muscat de Beaumes de Venise with the softened butter, and then rub this mixture over the birds. Leave them to marinate for 1 hour at room temperature.

Preheat the oven to 220°C/425°F/gas mark 7. Remove the tough outer leaves of the radicchio then rinse under cool water and lay on a tea towel to dry. Slice the radicchio into eight wedges, then brush the cut sides with oil and season with salt. Heat a large frying pan over a medium–high heat. Once hot, place the radicchio cut-side down in the pan and cook for about 5 minutes or until lightly charred. Then, transfer the radicchio to an ovenproof dish. Next place the marinated quails, breast side down, into the same pan (you may need to do this in two batches). Cook until the skin is browned all over then remove them and lay them, breast side up, on top of the radicchio. Slide the dish into the oven and cook for 6 minutes. To check if the quails are done, pierce the flesh just under the wing and, if it is pink, return it to the oven for 2 minutes more. Transfer the quails to a plate and allow to rest in a warm spot for 10 minutes.

Meanwhile, add the grapes to a roasting tray with the bay leaf and a second measure of muscat wine. Roast in the oven for 8 minutes until the grapes are slightly blistered and releasing their juices. Remove from the oven and add the balsamic vinegar. Shuffle the pan to mix things up.

Transfer the radicchio to a warm platter along with half of the grapes. Place the quails on top of the radicchio and add the rest of the grapes. Pour over any remaining juices and serve immediately.

PERSIMMON PAIRINGS

NUTS	*Almond, hazelnut, pecan, walnuts*
FLOWERS	*Orange blossom, rose*
SPICES	*Black pepper, cinnamon, clove, ginger, nutmeg, vanilla*
FRUIT	*Orange, pear, pomegranate*
VEGETABLES	*Beetroot, carrot, chicory, endive, radicchio, salad leaf*
FLOURS	*Spelt, white*
WINES AND SPIRITS	*Sherry, bourbon, brandy, Calvados, Grand Marnier, rum*
DAIRY	*Burrata, cream, crème fraîche, cheese, feta, ricotta, sheep's milk cheese*
OTHER FLAVOURS	*Coffee, caramel, olive oil, honey, sherry vinegar*

FAVOURITE COMBINATIONS WITH PERSIMMON

ORANGE BLOSSOM • SPELT | CINNAMON • BOURBON | RICOTTA • HONEY
PEAR • POMEGRANATE | ORANGE • CRÈME FRAÎCHE | VANILLA • CREAM

Dried Persimmons

When drying persimmons, I prefer to use non-astringent varieties, such as Fuyu, that are slightly more mature but still firm enough to maintain their shape when sliced. Underripe persimmons lack sufficient flavour, while overripe ones become mushy and lose their form. Therefore, this is an ideal project if you have an excess of ripe persimmons or if the persimmons in your fruit bowl are beginning to give.

MAKES 500G (1LB 2OZ)

5–6 persimmons

Prepare your dehydrator trays or an oven-safe wire rack. (Note you can still dehydrate persimmons on pieces of baking parchment or a silicone baking mat, but you will need to rotate the slices every couple of hours to ensure even drying.)

If you are drying the persimmons in your oven, set it to 70°C/160°F/gas mark as low as it will go.

Wash and dry the persimmons, then slice across the equator into even circles about 6cm (2½in) thick. Lay side by side on trays and place into the oven/dehydrator.

Have a peek at the persimmons after 4 hours, then every following hour to check their progress. They could take anywhere from 6–10 hours depending on the oven, thickness of the slices and how many trays you are dehydrating at the same time. The persimmons are done once they have become leathery, and the edges start to curl.

Serving suggestions: Serve with slices of firm sheep's milk cheese, or use them as a replacement for the pears in the Pear and Farro Salad with Radicchio and Walnuts (page 234) or chop into quarters and fold into the Persimmon Salad with Honeyed Walnuts and Burrata (page 200) for added texture.

Persimmon Salad with Honeyed Walnuts and Burrata

Firm, non-astringent persimmons lend themselves well to many different salads in autumn. The addition of burrata makes this dish feel more substantial and is therefore suitable for a light lunch or first course. The season for persimmons often aligns with the season for fresh walnuts, and if you happen to find any at the market, then use them in place of the honeyed walnuts.

SERVES 4

1 shallot, finely diced

2 tablespoons sherry or red wine vinegar

150g (5½oz) burrata

1 teaspoon wholegrain mustard

1 tablespoon walnut oil (or more olive oil)

2 tablespoons olive oil

2 persimmons, such as Fuyu

1 small head of radicchio or other chicory, leaves separated, then washed and dried

50g (1¾oz) mixed salad leaves, picked, washed and dried

90g (3¼oz) pomegranate seeds

75g (2½oz) Honeyed Walnuts (see opposite

salt and pepper

Place the diced shallot into a small bowl with the sherry vinegar and a pinch of salt. Leave for 15 minutes.

Meanwhile, tear the burrata over a bowl into four pieces and lightly season the cheese with salt and pepper. Whisk the mustard into the shallots, then slowly whisk in the walnut oil, followed by the olive oil.

Slice the persimmons into wedges the width of your smallest finger and set aside. Place the radicchio leaves into a wide bowl and dress with three-quarters of the shallot vinaigrette. Gently fold in the salad leaves, followed by the persimmon wedges, pomegranate seeds and half of the honeyed walnuts. Taste and adjust with vinegar or salt. Divide the torn burrata between four plates and distribute the salad. Finish with more vinaigrette if needed and the remaining honeyed walnuts.

Honeyed Walnuts

SERVES 4

70g (2½oz) honey
80g (2¾oz) caster sugar
50ml (1¾fl oz) water
large pinch of salt
250g (9oz) walnuts,
 lightly toasted and skins
 removed

Preheat the oven to 160°C/325°F/gas mark 3 and line a baking tray with a silicone mat or baking parchment.

Place the honey, sugar, water and salt into a saucepan large enough to hold the walnuts later. Put the pan over a medium heat and bring to the boil. Place a sieve over a bowl and set aside. Once the mixture begins to simmer, add the walnuts and toss several times to coat them. Remove from heat and transfer to the sieve to drain the excess liquid. Scatter the walnuts on the baking tray and bake for 15 minutes, stirring every so often to prevent clumping. If the nuts look wet on the parchment after 15 minutes, remove from the oven and quickly transfer the nuts to fresh parchment and bake for another 10–15 minutes until golden. Remove from the oven and leave to cool at room temperature before storing in an airtight container for up to a week. If they become soft or tacky, simply reheat in an oven for 5–7 minutes until crisp.

VARIATIONS

Honeyed Walnuts and Seeds: Substitute 25 g (1¾oz) of walnuts for a mixture of seeds, such as pumpkin, sunflower or sesame. Continue with the recipe as above. This is particularly good with thick yoghurt and Any Berry Compote (page 109), or scattered over lettuces dressed in Lemon and Buttermilk Dressing (page 44).

Spiced Pecans: Replace the walnuts with pecans. Make a spice mix by combining ½ teaspoon of ground cinnamon, ¼ teaspoon of ground cloves and ¼ teaspoon freshly grated nutmeg. After you have strained the nuts from the hot syrup, toss the pecans with the spice mix, then spread on a baking tray and continue with the recipe. Serve with Caramelized Apples (page 215), Poached Quinces (page 28) or on a plate with Candied Citrus Peel (page 54) for an after-dinner treat.

Steamed Persimmon Pudding

Made with silky persimmon pulp and warm spices, this pudding has a distinct flavour and moist texture. Choose an astringent variety of persimmon, such as Kaki or Hachiya, that has ripened completely, and make sure your spices are fresh. While persimmon pudding is rooted in American cuisine, this steamed version is decidedly British in style.

SERVES 8–10

90g (3oz) plain flour
1 teaspoon ground cinnamon
1 teaspoon salt
1¼ teaspoons bicarbonate of soda
160g (5½oz) persimmon purée (see page 14)
75g (2¾oz) unsalted butter, plus extra for greasing
190g (6¾oz) caster sugar
2 eggs
zest and juice of ½ orange
30g (1oz) dried currants or sultanas, soaked in 4 teaspoons brandy
65g (2½oz) lightly toasted walnuts, chopped

Begin by buttering a 450g (1lb) pudding basin.

Combine the flour, cinnamon and salt, then set aside. Stir the bicarbonate of soda into the persimmon purée, then, in a separate bowl, cream the butter and sugar until light and fluffy. Beat in the eggs, one by one, then follow with the persimmon purée, orange zest and juice. Fold in the dry ingredients, followed by the currants, brandy and toasted walnuts. Tip the batter into your pudding basin.

Cut a large circle of baking parchment that hangs halfway down the sides of the basin. Fold a pleat in the middle of the parchment and cover the top of the pudding basin. Tie a string twice around the rim of the basin, making it watertight, then make a loop over the top to form a handle. Place the basin into a large pan, and fill with enough boiling water to come two-thirds of the way up the sides. Place a lid over the top and steam for 2½ –3 hours. Cool on a wire rack, then cover and store at room temperature overnight. The following day, turn the pudding out onto a plate and slice into wedges and serve. If you wish to serve it warm, then set the oven to 150°C/300°F/gas mark 2, wrap the pudding in foil, and reheat for 25–30 minutes.

Serving suggestions: Serve with lightly whipped cream spiked with brandy (follow the recipe for Kirsch Cream on page 145, using regular brandy) and Candied Citrus Peel (page 54) or crème fraîche and Blood Oranges in Caramel (page 50).

POME FRUIT

APPLE, PEAR, QUINCE

Apples, pears and quinces are pome fruit, meaning they have a central core that contains their seeds. They all belong to the Malinae subtribe of the larger rose family, Rosaceae. I am often reminded of this connection when the first harvest of apples appears at the market. Apples have a delightful floral aroma that can only be experienced when freshly plucked from the tree in late summer and early autumn. Quinces possess it too, emitting a heady aroma that can fill an entire room. Pears, on the other hand, have a more delicate fragrance, complementing the sweet and subtle taste of their buttery flesh. These alluring qualities make apples, pears and quinces remarkably versatile to cook with. You can play with the light, mouthwatering acidity of a fresh apple by pairing it with lemon, honey or Tokaji, the famous dessert wine of Hungary. Alternatively, you can create a warm dish with pears using richer flavours like brown sugar or brandy.

Quinces are less common than apples or pears, but you can find them available for several months in autumn. Expect a few bruises and scrapes but avoid fruits with soft, large dark spots. Like pears, quinces ripen from the inside out, so later in the season, you might find fruit that's past its prime after they've been cut open. Although apples and pears can be enjoyed raw, cooking is required to unlock the flavour of quinces, which can be roasted in honey for a salad, or cooked in red wine and spices and served warm.

APPLE PAIRINGS

NUTS	Almond, chestnut, hazelnut, pecan, walnut
FLOWERS, LEAVES AND HERBS	Geranium, lavender, rose, sweet cicely, bay leaf, thyme
SPICES	Cardamom, cinnamon, clove, ginger, vanilla
FRUIT	Blackberry, cranberry, currant, elderberry, huckleberry, lemon, pear, prune, raspberry, raisin, rhubarb, quince
VEGETABLES	Cabbage, celeriac, celery, endive, fennel, radicchio, tomato, tomatillo, winter squash
FLOURS	Buckwheat, oat, plain, spelt, whole wheat
ALCOHOL	Armagnac, brandy, Calvados, dark rum, dry cider, mead, Poire Williams, sherry, Sauternes, Tokaji, whisky
DAIRY	Brown butter, aged sheep's milk, butter, Cheddar, Comté, cream, firm blues like Stilton, Gruyère
OTHER FLAVOURS	Butterscotch, caramel, honey, mustard, treacle

FAVOURITE COMBINATIONS WITH APPLE

CHICKEN • CALVADOS | BLACKBERRY • ROSE | LEMON • VANILLA • BUTTERMILK
BLUE CHEESE • HONEY • TOKAJI | PRUNE • ARMAGNAC • CRÈME FRAÎCHE
ENDIVE • WALNUT | CELERIAC • MUSTARD | CIDER • BUTTERSCOTCH
HAZELNUT • BROWN BUTTER | RHUBARB • ALMOND | CHEDDAR • SPELT
CINNAMON • PECAN • OAT | RAISIN • SPICED RUM | BUTTERMILK • CHIVES

Delicata Soup with Apples, Brown Butter and Fried Sage

Delicata is a Kabocha-type squash and the two resemble each other in their greyish-green skin and deep-orange flesh. To me, the two can be used interchangeably. If you cannot source either, then look out for onion squash (also called Red Kuri). This can also be made successfully with butternut squash.

SERVES 4

1 Delicata squash or 2
   small onion squash
olive oil
1 large onion, diced
3 carrots, peeled and diced
2 garlic cloves, diced
1 bay leaf
2 sprigs of sage, plus
   3–4 stems for garnish
   (optional)
pinch of chilli flakes
50g (1¾oz) unsalted butter
1 apple, peeled, quartered
   and cored
500–600ml (18–20fl oz)
   vegetable or chicken
   stock (preferably
   homemade)
salt and pepper

Preheat the oven to 200°C/400°F/gas mark 6.

Slice the squash in half and season the flesh with salt and pepper. Drizzle with olive oil and place the halves, cut-side down, on a roasting tray. Roast in the oven for 25–40 minutes until the skin becomes blistered and the flesh turns tender throughout. Once done, remove from the oven and allow to cool slightly.

In the meantime, take a large heavy-based saucepan and add a drizzle of olive oil, along with the onions and carrots. Sprinkle a pinch of salt over them and cook over a low heat with the lid on for about 10 minutes until the onions become translucent without browning. Stir in the garlic, bay leaf, sage and chilli flakes then continue to cook for a further 10 minutes.

While the vegetables cook, make the brown butter. Place the butter in a stainless-steel-based (or other light-coloured) pan over a medium heat. Once the butter has melted and started to foam, gently swirl the pan and scrape the bottom where the solids are beginning to settle. After a few minutes, the butter will begin to colour. Reduce the heat so the foam settles and continue to cook until the butter solids are hazelnut brown. Immediately transfer the butter to a heatproof bowl and keep somewhere warm.

Once the squash has cooled enough to handle, remove the seeds and stringy core. Scoop out the soft flesh and add it to the pan along with the apple, stock and half the brown butter. Set aside the remaining brown butter for later. Increase the heat to medium–high and bring everything to the boil, then reduce the heat slightly and continue to simmer for about 20 minutes until the apple is soft.

Recipe continued overleaf

Remove the pan from the heat and discard the bay leaf. Transfer one-third of the soup to a blender, and purée until smooth. Be careful when blending hot liquids, as pressure can build up and cause the lid to come off unexpectedly. To avoid this, fill the blender jug no more than halfway, and leave the lid slightly ajar, allowing the steam to escape. Placing a tea towel over the top will catch any potential splatters. Once the soup is smooth, pour it into a large bowl and continue with the other two-thirds. Return the blended soup to the pan (it may require reheating), then taste and adjust the seasoning to your preference.

If you wish to garnish the soup with fried sage, take a small frying pan and pour in enough olive oil to cover the base. Place the pan over medium–high heat. Set aside 12 sage leaves. Line a heatproof ceramic plate with kitchen paper and keep it nearby. After a minute or two, test the temperature of the oil by adding a drop of water; if it sizzles, add the sage leaves. Let them fry for around 2–3 seconds, then turn off the heat. Allow the sage to fry for a few more seconds, then transfer it to the prepared kitchen paper to drain. Season the fried sage while it's still hot, then let it cool.

When you are ready to serve, check to see if the remaining brown butter is still melted, if not, gently warm through. Ladle the warm soup into bowls and swirl in spoonfuls of brown butter. Finish with freshly ground pepper and the fried sage, if using.

Crab Cakes with Apple and Fennel Salad

These crab cakes are seasoned with fresh herbs, zesty lemon, and a subtle touch of chilli. The accompanying apple and fennel salad adds a refreshing crunch. Together they create a well balanced, satisfying meal.

SERVES 4

For the crab cakes
olive oil
50g (1¾oz) flat-leaf parsley (or a mix of parsley, chervil and fennel fronds)
2 garlic cloves
200g (7oz) halibut fillet, bones removed
2 celery sticks, finely diced
1 outer layer of fennel bulb (from the apple salad below), finely diced
3 spring onions
300g (10½oz) picked crab meat (from 1 large or 2 medium freshly cooked crabs)
30g (1oz) dried breadcrumbs
200g (7oz) Homemade Mayonnaise (page 44), plus extra to serve
½ teaspoon chilli flakes
zest and juice of 1 lemon
salt and pepper

Select a pan large enough to fit the halibut. Pour 300ml (10fl oz) of water along with 50ml (1¾fl oz) of olive oil and 2 teaspoons of salt. Place the pan over a medium–low heat.

Meanwhile, pluck the parsley leaves, setting aside the stems. Transfer the leaves to a small bowl and cover with a damp kitchen paper, then place into the refrigerator for later. Add the stems and 1 whole clove of garlic to the poaching liquid. Once the liquid begins to boil, reduce the heat slightly and carefully slip the halibut into the pan. Cover with a lid and poach the halibut for 10 minutes until the flesh is flaky and thoroughly cooked. Remove the halibut from the liquid and cool to room temperature.

While the halibut cools, finely chop the second garlic clove and place it in a bowl along with the diced celery and fennel. Finely chop the green stems of the spring onions and add them to the bowl of vegetables. Then finely chop the white bulbs of the spring onions and place them in a separate bowl.

Place a sauté pan over medium–low heat and add a couple of spoonfuls of oil. Add the chopped celery, fennel and spring onion stems to the pan, season with salt, and cover. Reduce the heat to low, and cook for about 15 minutes until the vegetables become soft and translucent. Transfer the cooked mixture to a bowl and allow it to cool to room temperature.

In a large bowl, combine the celery mixture with the chopped fresh spring onions. Add the crab, breadcrumbs, mayonnaise, chilli flakes and the lemon zest and juice. Chop the reserved parsley leaves and break the halibut into small pieces, then add both to the bowl and mix everything together. Taste and adjust the seasoning.

Ingredients and recipe continued overleaf

For coating and frying

plain flour

2 eggs, beaten

200g (7oz) dried
  breadcrumbs

olive oil

butter

For the apple salad

1 fennel bulb, quartered
  and thinly sliced

4 leafy celery sticks, sliced
  diagonally 5mm (¼in)
  thick

1 crisp apple, quartered,
  cored and sliced 5mm
  (¼in) thick

3 tablespoons Simple
  Vinaigrette (page 148)

lemon juice

more soft herbs, such as
  fennel, chervil or parsley
  (optional)

To shape the crab cakes, prepare a plate with flour and place the beaten eggs into a bowl. Scatter the breadcrumbs on another plate and arrange all three in a line. Weigh out portions of the crab mixture to 60g (2¼oz) and shape into little cakes. Start by coating one crab cake in flour, then tap off as much of the excess flour as possible. Dip it in the beaten egg, followed by the breadcrumbs. Repeat this process for the same crab cake, ensuring you remove any excess flour, so that it is double coated in the flour, egg and breadcrumbs. Do the same with the remaining cakes, then place all the cakes into the refrigerator to chill for 30 minutes.

When you are ready to cook the crab cakes, heat 2 tablespoons of olive oil with 2 tablespoons of butter in a pan. Once the butter has melted and the oil begins to sizzle, slide the cakes into the pan. You may need to cook them in batches, allowing enough space between the cakes for browning. Cook each side for approximately 3–4 minutes until they turn golden and crisp. Flip the cakes to brown the other side, then place them on kitchen paper to drain the excess oil. Transfer them to a low oven to keep warm. Repeat the process with the remaining cakes, adding more butter and olive oil as needed.

For the salad, transfer the sliced fennel, celery and apple to a large bowl and toss them with the vinaigrette. Add a squeeze of lemon juice and a mix of soft herbs, then toss again.

To serve, plate two crab cakes alongside a portion of the salad. Provide a bowl of mayonnaise on the side.

VARIATIONS

In the height of citrus season, consider swapping the apple for clementines, blood oranges, grapefruits or a mix of all three.

Caramelized Apples Two Ways

You will want to use a variety of apple that holds up to cooking for this recipe. Pink Lady, Cox's and Braeburn are all excellent choices. If you happen to be purchasing your apples from a farmers' market, ask the farmer for their recommendation, since they know the characteristics of their own apples best. Select a sauté pan that is spacious enough to comfortably accommodate the sliced apples, and plan to cook them in batches. Overcrowding the pan with apples will result in steaming rather than caramelization, so it's best to cook the fruit in a single layer. The savoury apples accompany the Braised Pork Shoulder with Cider (page 217) and would even be nice over the Delicata Soup with Apples, Brown Butter and Fried Sage (page 209). Make the sweeter version for Buckwheat Crêpes (page 225) or to serve with Ginger Cake (page 90).

SERVES 4–6

SWEET
45g (1½oz) unsalted butter
3 large apples peeled, quartered, cored and sliced
1 tablespoon caster sugar
zest and juice of 1 lemon
2 tablespoons Calvados or brandy
candied lemon peel (optional)

In a large frying pan, heat half the butter over a medium–high heat. Once it begins to sizzle, add half the sliced apples and cook for 5–7 minutes. Flip the apples and sprinkle ½ tablespoon of sugar over them. Cook for another 5–6 minutes until the slices have softened and the sugar has caramelized. You may need to move the apples around the pan to ensure even browning. Once the apples are tender and caramelized, add half the lemon juice, zest and Calvados. Give the apples a few tosses in the pan, then transfer them to a plate and keep them warm. Wipe the pan clean and repeat with the remaining apples. Serve immediately with a scattering of candied lemon peel if desired.

SAVOURY
45g (1½oz) unsalted butter
3 large apples peeled, quartered, cored and sliced
½ teaspoon caster sugar
1 sprig of thyme
2 tablespoons Calvados or brandy
¼ teaspoon salt

In a large frying pan, heat half the butter over a medium–high heat. Once it begins to sizzle, add half the sliced apples and cook for 5–7 minutes. Flip the apples and sprinkle ¼ teaspoon sugar over them. Cook for another 5–6 minutes until the slices have softened and the sugar has caramelized. You may need to move the apples around the pan to ensure even browning. Once the apples are tender and caramelized, add half the thyme, Calvados and salt. Give the apples a few tosses in the pan, then transfer them to a plate and keep them warm. Wipe the pan clean and repeat with the remaining apples. Serve immediately.

Braised Pork Shoulder
with Cider and Caramelized Apples

This dish celebrates many prized ingredients of Normandy such as apples, cider and Calvados. Like many slow-cooked braises, this is more delicious and balanced the following day, so I have written the recipe that way. The dried chilli is untraditional and totally optional but I added it because the pork called for it. Whatever you do, don't skip the vinegar, it cuts through the richness and brightens the dish.

SERVES 6

2kg (4lb 8oz) pork
    shoulder, deboned, but
    skin and fat still attached
2 onions, sliced
½ head of garlic, unpeeled
1 bay leaf
1 dried chilli (optional)
2 sprigs of sage
300ml (10fl oz) dry apple
    cider
2 tablespoons apple cider
    vinegar
1 tablespoon Calvados
2 teaspoons wholegrain
    mustard
1 quantity Savoury
    Caramelized Apples
    (page 215)
salt and pepper

Generously season the pork shoulder all over with salt and pepper. Leave for at least 1 hour or store overnight in the refrigerator. (If refrigerating, bring up to room temperature before cooking.)

Preheat the oven to 160°C/325°F/gas mark 3.

In a large, lidded, cast-iron casserole, make a bed of sliced onions, garlic, bay leaf, dried chilli (if using) and sage, then place the pork shoulder on top. Add the cider, vinegar and just enough water to submerge the pork three-quarters of the way up. Cover and place over a medium–high heat. When the liquid begins to boil, transfer the casserole with its lid to the preheated oven. Cook for 30 minutes, then carefully turn the pork and put it back into the oven. Continue to cook, turning the meat every 30–45 minutes and add more cider or water if the braise looks dry. The pork is ready when the meat is tender and easily pulls apart, usually 4–5 hours. Take the casserole out of the oven, remove the lid and allow it to cool to room temperature. Place the lid back on top and transfer the dish to the refrigerator overnight.

The next day, skim the fat off the top of the broth, reserving 3 tablespoons for frying the pork. Gently warm the pork and broth on the hob, then remove the pork onto a plate and pat dry with a kitchen towel. Strain the broth through a colander, pushing the solids with a spatula or spoon to extract as much flavour as possible. Warm the reserved pork fat in a large frying pan over a medium–high heat and, when the fat begins to sizzle, add the pork and brown on all sides. Pour the strained broth back into the casserole with the Calvados and mustard. When the pork is crisp and well coloured, return it to the broth and bring to the boil, then reduce it to a simmer. Gently cook the broth, basting the pork every few minutes or so, until the liquid is reduced by half. Taste and adjust the seasoning if necessary. Transfer the pork to a serving platter and scatter the warm caramelized apples over the top. Finish with the sauce and serve immediately.

Apple, Prune and Armagnac Tart

This variation of apple tart, with its simplicity and sophistication, offers a burst of flavour from the prunes and Armagnac. Through my experience, I've noticed that different apples can behave differently even under the same baking conditions. So, it's wise to keep a watchful eye on the tart as it bakes. Should the apples start to dry out, a gentle brush of butter can revive them. Should they begin to brown too quickly, cover with a piece of baking parchment or reduce the oven temperature slightly. Most of the sweetness in this dessert comes from the prune purée and the glaze. However, a bit of sugar over the apples will help them to soften and colour. For an added touch of sweetness, serve it with Prunes in Armagnac Caramel (page 249).

SERVES 10–12

For the flaky pastry
270g (9¾oz) cold butter, cubed, plus extra for greasing
400g (14oz) plain flour, plus extra for dusting
115g (4oz) ice-cold water

For the filling
1 quantity of Prunes in Armagnac Caramel (page 249)
5 medium apples
1 scant tablespoon caster sugar
20g (¾oz) unsalted butter, melted

To prepare the flaky pastry, combine the butter with the flour in a container and chill in the refrigerator for a minimum of 30 minutes.

Once the flour and butter have sufficiently chilled, take them out of the refrigerator and transfer them to a food processor. Pulse a few times until the butter is the size of peas. Measure the ice-cold water and, with the motor running, pour the water in a steady stream into the processor. Stop while the dough is loose and the texture of fine breadcrumbs but comes together when squeezed in the palm of your hand. If there are any wet patches, simply break them up with the tips of your fingers, then pulse the machine a few more times. Tip the dough onto a clean surface and bring it together using a dough scraper or your hands. Divide into two rounds and wrap in baking parchment. Using your knuckles, shape the dough into two discs, smoothing out the edges with your thumbs to prevent cracking. Cover and refrigerate for at least 2 hours, or preferably overnight. You will only need one dough for the tart, so if you want to freeze the other one, refrigerate overnight and freeze the following day.

On the day before baking the tart, lightly butter a 23cm (9in) fluted tart tin with a removable base. Unwrap the pastry and lightly dust both sides with flour. Place the dough between two sheets of baking parchment and, starting from the centre, roll it outwards. Give the dough a quarter turn and continue rolling, repeating the turning and rolling process until it forms an even circle with a diameter of approximately 27cm (10½in). If the dough proves difficult to roll, let it rest on the work surface for 5 minutes to soften. If it feels too soft or sticky, return it to the refrigerator before continuing. To transfer the dough to the tart tin, remove the top parchment and lightly dust the surface of the dough. Bring the tart tin next to you, then roll the dough onto the rolling pin. Lift the rolling pin over the tart tin, then unroll the dough over it, using your fingers to press the dough into the tart tin and evenly up the sides. Trim the edges and put into the refrigerator to chill.

Ingredients and recipe continued overleaf

For the glaze

apple cores and peel (from those used for the filling)

100ml (3½fl oz) unfiltered apple juice

100ml (3½fl oz) prune-Armagnac soaking liquid

1 tablespoon caster sugar

splash of Armagnac

To serve

crème fraîche or cold double cream

1 quantity of Prunes in Armagnac Caramel (page 249)

The next day, preheat the oven to 170°C/340°F/gas mark 3½ . Remove the tart shell from the refrigerator and line with a piece of baking parchment and pie weights, rice or baking beans. Bake for 20–25 minutes until lightly golden and cooked all the way through. Remove from the oven and place it on a wire rack. Carefully remove the pie weights and parchment, which will still be hot, and allow the tart shell to cool before filling. Increase the oven temperature to 190°C/375°F/gas mark 5, and place an inverted baking tray onto the middle rack.

To prepare the filling, strain the prunes over a bowl and keep the poaching liquid aside (this will be used for the glaze). Place the prunes on a clean chopping board and roughly chop them into a purée-like consistency. They should be soft and easily fall apart. Once the tart shell has cooled, scatter the prune purée around the base of the tart. Using the back of a spoon or a small palette knife, evenly spread the purée across the tart shell and set aside. Peel, quarter and core the apples, reserving the peels and cores for the glaze. Take one apple quarter and finely chop it into small chunks. Sprinkle these chunks evenly over the prune filling and add a teaspoon of sugar.

Slice the remaining apple quarters lengthwise and create a decorative pattern as you layer them into the tart shell. The fruit will shrink slightly while baking, so feel free to be generous when covering the filling. Brush the apples with the melted butter and sprinkle the remaining sugar on top. Bake the tart on top of the inverted baking tray for 25 minutes. Then rotate it and bake for an additional 20–25 minutes.

While the tart is baking, make the glaze. Place the apple peel and cores into a pan with the apple juice and 100ml (3½fl oz) of water. Bring to the boil, then simmer for 30 minutes. Strain the liquid, then return to the saucepan with the reserved prune liquid and 1 tablespoon of sugar. Bring back to the boil and reduce until the glaze coats the back of a spoon. Remove from the heat, transfer to a bowl and stir in the Armagnac. Allow to cool completely.

To check if the tart is done, taste one of the apple slices. It should be tender, brown around the edge and without any crunchiness. Once the tart is thoroughly baked, take it out of the oven and place it on a wire rack. While the apples are still hot, brush them with glaze to prevent drying, then let the tart cool for 20 minutes. Serve it slightly warm (not hot), or allow it to cool until it reaches room temperature. Before slicing, apply another brush of glaze, and enjoy with crème fraîche and one or two Prunes in Armagnac Caramel.

VARIATIONS

Apple and Quince Tart: Pulse 225g (8oz) Poached Quinces (page 28) and spread over the bottom of the tart in place of the prune purée. Substitute 1–2 of the apples with poached quinces when slicing, and as you layer the fruit, place one slice of poached quince for every three slices of apple. Reduce the quince poaching liquid until syrupy and use it in place of the prune glaze.

Apple and Mincemeat Tart: Spread 225g (8oz) Mincemeat (page 243) on the bottom of the tart in place of the prune purée. Omit the prune liquid from the glaze, adding ¼ teaspoon of grated nutmeg instead.

Apple and Blackberry Tart: Scatter 1 tablespoon of ground almonds over the bottom of the tart base. Spread 200g (7oz) chopped blackberries in place of the prunes and sprinkle with 1 teaspoon of sugar. Proceed with the chopped apples, then the sliced apples. Omit the prune liquid from the glaze, then gently toss a large handful of blackberries in the remaining glaze and dot around the finished tart.

Apple, Prune and Armagnac Tart

COOKING STARTS IN THE GARDEN

A cook will learn a lot about food by stepping out of the kitchen and into the garden. Growing your own food – whether on a windowsill, a front porch or in the ground – provides direct access to ingredients that are vibrant and alive, which in turn will improve your cooking. It is one of the best ways to engage with the seasons and the soil, reminding us that nature decides what food is made of, not the food industry.

It is easy enough to begin with a pot of commonly used herbs like parsley, mint or rosemary. In my own garden, I often plant soft herbs that are difficult to source in supermarkets but grow well in a small space, like chervil, anise hyssop and sweet cicely. I also like to grow the more fragile leaves like lemon verbena, roses (cultivated for fragrance) and scented geraniums, all of which I use for steeping in creams and syrups (see Cooking with Aromatic Leaves and Flowers, page 189). Their vibrancy inspires me more than any fancy ingredient bought at a specialist store.

PEAR PAIRINGS

NUTS AND SEEDS	*Almond, chestnut, hazelnut, pecan, pistachio, walnut, pine nut*
FLOWERS	*Chamomile, geranium, rose*
SPICES	*Anise, cardamom, cinnamon, ginger, vanilla*
FRUITS	*Apple, autumn raspberry, blackberry, cranberry, date, elderberry, fig, grape, persimmon, pomegranate, prune, raisin, quince*
VEGETABLES	*Cabbage, celery, endive, fennel, radicchio, rocket*
FLOURS	*Chestnut, oat, rye, spelt*
ALCOHOL	*Brandy, Chartreuse, cider, marsala, pear cider, Poire Williams, red wine, Vin Santo, white wine*
DAIRY AND MEAT	*Aged pecorino, Camembert, goat's cheese, mellow blue cheese, bacon, duck, pork, quail*
OTHER FLAVOURS	*Brown butter, butterscotch, chocolate, honey, farro, coffee espresso*

FAVOURITE COMBINATIONS WITH PEAR

ALMOND • RASPBERRY | HAZELNUT • COFFEE ESPRESSO | ENDIVE • WALNUT

BLACKBERRY • POIRE WILLIAMS | BROWN BUTTER • CHESTNUT

CAMEMBERT • CHESTNUT | QUAIL • WALNUT | PECORINO • HONEY

Buckwheat Crêpes
with Roasted Pears and Marsala

Pears and marsala are often cooked together, but I like their singular flavours served side by side. The recipe for the crêpes will yield at least eight large portions with plenty of room for error. Any extra crêpes can be enjoyed with a few thin slices of high-quality ham and Gruyère cheese, heated in the oven until the cheese has melted and the edges turn crisp.

SERVES 8

For the buckwheat crêpes
270ml (9½fl oz) full-fat milk
65g (2¼oz) unsalted butter
1½ teaspoons salt
1½ teaspoons sugar
115g (4oz) buckwheat flour
70g (2½oz) wholemeal
  spelt flour
70g (2½oz) plain flour
195g (7oz) eggs (3–4 eggs),
  at room temperature
1½ teaspoons grapeseed
  oil
200ml (7fl oz) beer
clarified butter, for cooking
  (see Note overleaf)

For the roasted pears
5 pears
60g (2¼oz) unsalted butter
150ml (5fl oz) water
4 tablespoons marsala
55g (2oz) caster sugar
1½ tablespoons icing sugar
1 tablespoon Poire
  Williams (optional)

For the crêpes, gently warm 170ml (6fl oz) of the milk in a small saucepan with the butter, salt, and sugar until the butter melts. Allow the mixture to cool to room temperature. In a wide bowl, combine all the flours and whisk them together. In a separate bowl, whisk the eggs, oil and cooled milk until smooth. Create a well in the flour mixture and gradually whisk the wet ingredients into the dry until all the flour is incorporated. Finally, whisk in the beer. Cover the batter and refrigerate it overnight. The following day, remove the batter from the refrigerator and stir in the remaining 100ml (3½fl oz) milk until the batter reaches the consistency of thick buttermilk (you may not need it all).

To cook the crêpes, heat a well-seasoned 20 or 23cm (8 or 9in) crêpe pan, cast-iron pan, or frying pan over a medium heat. Swirl about ½ teaspoon of clarified butter until foamy, then pour out any excess. Ladle approximately 4 tablespoons of batter into the pan and swirl to create a thin pancake. Cook the crêpe for 1–1½ minutes until golden brown on the first side, then flip and cook for another 30 seconds on the second side. Don't be discouraged if the first crêpe sticks. In fact, I often 'sacrifice' the first crêpe to check the heat of the pan and the batter's thickness. If it is taking longer than 3 minutes to cook, then consider increasing the heat or adding less batter to the pan. If the crêpe starts to burn, then reduce the heat and try again. Slide the crêpe onto a large plate and continue with the remaining batter. If at any point the crêpes begin to stick to the pan, add a tad more butter. Wipe away any excess butter or burnt bits of batter as you go.

Cover the crêpes with kitchen paper, followed by a tea towel and leave at room temperature for an hour or two to cool completely. Then cover well and store at room temperature for up to 2 days. To freeze, wait until the crêpes are completely cool, then stack between pieces of baking parchment and store in a sealed container. Bring to room temperature before using.

Recipe continued overleaf

Pome Fruit

For the marsala ice cream

Plain Ice Cream Base (page 16)

200ml (7fl oz) sweet marsala

To serve

150g (5½oz) unsalted butter, softened

50g (1¾oz) icing sugar, plus extra for dusting

zest of 1 lemon

3 tablespoons sweet marsala

NOTE:

Clarified butter is ideal for cooking crêpes, thanks to its higher smoke point. To make clarified butter, start by placing 500g (17½oz) of unsalted butter into a pan and bring to a boil. As the butter heats, you'll notice milk solids rising to the surface – skim off and discard the foam, then reduce the heat to a gentle simmer and continue cooking for 5 minutes. Remove the pan from the heat and carefully strain the butter through a cheesecloth or a coffee filter into a heatproof container. When properly sealed, clarified butter can be stored for up to six months.

To make the marsala ice cream, stir the marsala into the ice cream base and taste. Adjust the marsala and sugar to your liking, then churn the mixture in an ice-cream maker following the manufacturer's instructions.

For the roasted pears, preheat the oven to 220°C/425°F/gas mark 7. Slice the pears in half, then slice each half into three slices, so that each pear gives you six slices. Carve out the core. If your pears seem a little firm, then place the cored slices into a bowl with a squeeze of lemon and a dash of Poire Williams. Leave to soften for at least 30 minutes, tossing every 10 minutes or so.

In a saucepan, combine the butter, water, marsala and sugar and bring to the boil, stir to dissolve the sugar, then remove from the heat. Place the pears, cut-side down, into a baking dish large enough for them to fit comfortably in an even layer. Pour the liquid evenly over the fruit. Dust the fruit with icing sugar and sprinkle with Poire Williams (if using). Cover tightly with foil, then place into the oven. Bake for 10–15 minutes until the fruit begins to soften. Remove the foil and turn the fruit cut-side up. Continue cooking, uncovered, for 10 minutes until the fruit begins to colour and the sauce below bubbles and thickens slightly. The pears should be soft and slightly caramelized at the edges, the sauce should be spoonable, but glossy. If the fruit is still firm, bake a little longer. If the sauce is thin after the fruit is cooked, strain off the liquid and boil until you have a glossy texture. Remove from the heat and cool slightly.

To serve, preheat the oven to 200°C/400°F/gas mark 6.

Beat the butter, icing sugar and lemon zest together. Cut each crêpe in half, then smear each half with 1 tablespoon of the lemon butter. Fold into thirds and place into a baking dish then continue with the other crêpes and lemon butter. Splash the marsala over the top, then cook for 2–3 minutes until all the crêpes are warmed through. Serve two crêpes per serving with a few warm roasted pears. Spoon over the juices from the roasted pears and finish with a scoop of marsala ice cream.

Hazelnut and Pear Cake with Espresso

This recipe is inspired by one of the first desserts featured on the opening menu at Spring in 2014 – a hazelnut and pear tart. Here I have presented it in the form of a cake. Fresh grounds of espresso beans are scattered over the cake just before serving, though this is entirely optional. I enjoy this cake best when it is baked in a tart tin, which results in a higher fruit-to-cake ratio, and long, elegant slices.

SERVES 10–12

3–4 medium pears

2 tablespoons Poire Williams or cognac (optional)

juice of ¼ lemon

40g (1½oz) plain flour

1 teaspoon baking powder

½ teaspoon salt

30g (1oz) cornflour

200g (7oz) hazelnuts, toasted, skins removed

100g (3½oz) almond flour

200g (7oz) caster sugar

155g (5½oz) unsalted butter, softened, plus extra for greasing

4 eggs

2 tablespoons demerara sugar

freshly ground espresso or coffee beans (optional)

crème fraîche, soured cream or yoghurt, to serve

Preheat the oven to 160°C/325°F/gas mark 3. Grease a 25cm (10in) tart tin with a removable base and line the bottom with baking parchment.

Halve the pears with their skins on, then slice each half into three, giving six slices per pear. Remove stems and cores, then toss the slices with Poire Williams and lemon juice in a bowl and set aside.

In a separate bowl, sift the flour, baking powder, salt and cornflour. Then in a food processor, blend 150g (5½oz) of the toasted hazelnuts with the almond flour and sugar until the hazelnuts are roughly broken. With the processor running, gradually add the butter and blend until the mixture is smooth and fluffy. Incorporate the eggs, one at a time, then scrape the sides and pulse the machine to mix well. Add the dry ingredients and pulse, then scrape, then pulse again just until everything is incorporated. Transfer the batter to the tin.

Arrange the slices on top of the batter in concentric circles. Coarsely chop the remaining 50g (1¾oz) of toasted hazelnuts and scatter over the top, then follow with demerara sugar. Bake for 45–50 minutes or until set, then allow it to cool on a wire rack. Serve with a sprinkle of freshly ground espresso and a dollop of crème fraîche.

PAIRING FRUIT WITH ESPRESSO FLAVOUR

The flavour of espresso complements many fruits surprisingly well. If you consider your favourite fruit-and-chocolate pairing, you'll likely find that the same fruit pairs well with espresso. This isn't surprising, given the shared characteristics between chocolate and espresso – both offer dark, roasted undertones with slightly nutty, and even fruity notes. My top fruit pairings with espresso include strawberries, cherries, pears, oranges and prunes.

IN THE WORDS OF THE FARMER

Mags Coughlan

Ballymaloe House, Cork, Ireland, Pears

Ballymaloe House has two acres of walled garden, growing organic fruit, vegetables and cut flowers for the restaurant. After over ten years in the role of Head Gardener, I can admit to loving my surroundings whatever the season. I have only ever gardened organically and am passionate about this way of growing. My role is closely linked to the kitchen so that I can supply them with seasonal, fresh produce all year around.

Each year, towards the end of the growing season, I meet with the chefs to review the year just passed and to plan for the coming year – we discuss new varieties, new ideas and volumes to be grown. This yearly meeting is important to both chefs and gardeners as we get to peruse seed catalogues and cookbooks to look at new vegetables, herbs and fruit and discuss whether they could be useful in the kitchen, or grown in our climate. They also mean that the chefs can see the vegetables at all growing stages – this year we started using spring onions at about 6cm (2⅓in) long, before they reached their full size, as an elegant, tasty garnish. Because of this, I now grow twice the quantity of spring onions and start harvesting well before they reach the potential size!

Space is at a premium in a walled garden so our fruit trees are 'restricted' through pruning – the stone walls provide support and protection for fan-trained, cordons and espaliered pears, apples, cherries, peaches and nectarines. As the autumn weather begins to make itself felt, the many pears growing begin to ripen – the ten varieties growing in the walled garden include the early ripening Jargonelle, Doyenne du Comice, Beth, Concorde, Beurre Hardy and late-storing Josephine de Malines. Knowing the best time to pick a pear varies depending on what book you read. Early-ripening pears will almost give a little when given a gentle squeeze, whereas a pear variety like Onward will often be picked when hard as a stone and will then ripen in a fruit bowl as the days go by. Personally, I wait until the pear stem breaks easily from the spur when moved to a 90-degree

angle. Occasionally, I'll grow a pear in a bottle and when the pear naturally breaks away from the stem, I fill the bottle with brandy and sip the pear-infused tipple during the cold winter.

My favourite dish is a distant memory of a starter I had in Cork city almost 15 years ago – it was a simple pear, Florence fennel and walnut salad. The pear was perfectly ripe and complemented the other ingredients and a lightly dressed salad. I've tried to recreate this dish without success so my next favourite would have to be the poached pears made by the Ballymaloe pastry team!

Pear and Brown Butter 'Butter'

Fruit butters fall into the same categories as jams and jellies but are often made using fruit with higher fibre and lower water content. For this reason, they typically require less sugar and shorter cooking times. What I particularly like about fruit butters is their ability to capture the flavour of a fruit without an overpowering sweetness. The addition of brown butter to pear adds a subtle nutty flavour.

MAKES 6 x 300G (10½OZ) JARS

1kg (2lb 4oz) pears, peeled, cored and diced
400g (14oz) caster sugar
50g (1¾oz) unsalted butter
½ vanilla pod, split and seeds removed

Begin by making the brown butter. Place the butter in a stainless-steel-based (or other light-coloured) saucepan over a medium heat. Once the butter is melted and begins to foam, gently swirl the pan and scrape the bottom where solids are beginning to settle. After a few minutes, the butter will begin to colour. Reduce the heat so the foam settles and continue to cook until the butter solids are hazelnut brown. Remove from the heat and strain into a heatproof bowl.

In a heavy-based saucepan, place the sliced fruit along with just enough water to completely cover the bottom of the pan. Cover the pan tightly and place over high heat for 4–5 minutes. As the fruit steams and softens, use a whisk to break it up, then stir in the brown butter, sugar and vanilla seeds. Meanwhile, place a small plate or saucer in the freezer.

Bring the mixture to a boil, then reduce the heat slightly and continue to cook over a medium heat, stirring occasionally to prevent the pear butter from catching on the bottom of the pan. Observe the changes in the texture as the liquid reduces. The bubbles will become larger, slower and less frequent.

After 20 minutes, check the set by removing the plate from the freezer and placing a spoonful of the pear butter on it, then returning to the freezer for 1 minute. If the pear butter holds its shape when you run your finger through it, it is set. If not, continue cooking for a few more minutes.

Ladle the hot butter into clean, sterilized jars. Use within 1–2 months. (See Notes on Making Jam, page 107.)

Pear and Farro Salad
with Radicchio and Walnuts

This grain salad strikes a perfect balance: it's both crunchy and creamy, blending sweet, nutty, bitter, and bright flavours.

SERVES 4

3 leafy celery sticks

300g (10½oz) pearled farro, spelt or barley (see Note)

2 tablespoons apple cider vinegar

1 bay leaf

½ head of radicchio

50g (1¾oz) walnuts, lightly toasted and skins removed

4 tablespoons Simple Vinaigrette (page 148)

2 ripe pears, such as Warren, Williams or Comice

15g (½oz) firm sheep's milk cheese, such as Ossau-Iraty, or a young pecorino

olive oil, for drizzling

salt and pepper

NOTE:

If you use unpearled grains, submerge them in plenty of salted water with the other aromatics and boil until they are tender and chewy. This may take 45 minutes–1 hour. Strain and continue with the recipe.

Rinse the celery under cool water, then chop the white ends off and reserve them for cooking with the farro. Pick the celery leaves and set aside as a garnish. Take the remaining celery sticks and finely dice them, then place into a bowl for later.

Place the farro, vinegar, bay leaf and the celery ends into a saucepan. Add a pinch of salt and 750ml (26fl oz) of water and bring to the boil. Reduce the heat to a gentle simmer and cover, then cook for about 20 minutes until the farro is tender and the liquid has been absorbed. Turn off the heat but keep covered, allowing the farro to steam.

While the farro is cooling, peel away the outer leaves of the radicchio, removing any that are damaged or tough. Continue to peel back the tender leaves, then wash, spin and gently dry on a clean tea towel. Coarsely chop the walnuts and set aside.

When the farro is cool enough to handle, remove the celery and bay leaf, then place the farro into a large bowl with the vinaigrette, celery and two-thirds of the walnuts. Slice the radicchio into thin strips, add it to the farro and toss to coat everything together.

Slice the pears into quarters. Remove the core, then slice each quarter in half from top to tail. You should have sixteen slices in total. Dice each slice into 3–4 chunks. Gently fold the pears through the salad, then follow with shavings of cheese, reserving a little for the end. Taste for seasoning and adjust if necessary. Place the salad on a platter and distribute the remaining walnuts and cheese over the top. Finish with the celery leaves and a drizzle of olive oil.

VARIATION

Swap the pears for apples, the walnuts for hazelnuts and the cheese for another hard variety like Cheddar, Parmesan or Beaufort.

Pear and Farro Salad with Radicchio and Walnuts

QUINCE PAIRINGS

NUTS AND SEEDS	*Almond, hazelnut, peacan, sesame, walnut*
FLOWERS, LEAVES AND HERBS	*Rose, rose hip, bay leaf, thyme, sage*
SPICES	*Cardamom, cinnamon, ginger, vanilla*
FRUITS	*Apple, blackberry, date, elderberry, orange, pear*
VEGETABLES	*Carrot, celeriac, chicory, Iceberg lettuce, potato, Romaine lettuce*
FLOURS	*Polenta, rye, semolina, spelt*
ALCOHOL	*Calvados, cider, Muscat, red wine, sherry, white wine*
DAIRY AND MEAT	*Buttermilk, crème fraîche, Manchego, Mascarpone, pecorino, Parmesan, yoghurt, young sheep's milk cheese, chicken, pork*
OTHER FLAVOURS	*Brown sugar, honey*

FAVOURITE COMBINATIONS WITH QUINCE

WALNUT • RYE | SHERRY • CREAM | APPLE • BRANDY | ORANGE • MASCARPONE
CELERIAC • POTATO | PORK • SAGE | SHEEP'S MILK CHEESE • SPELT
RASPBERRY • CRÈME FRAÎCHE | CHICKEN • BAY LEAF

Roast Chicken with Potatoes and Quince Aïoli

Quince Aïoli originates from northern Spain, near the border that nudges into the Pyrenees, where the cooler climate is favourable for growing quince. Traditionally, it is made with membrillo, a Spanish quince paste. However, if quince is thoroughly poached, it is possible to achieve the same deep, reddish colour that is characteristic of traditional membrillo. Here, the aïoli is served alongside the classic chicken and chips.

SERVES 4

1.2–1.4kg (2lb 10oz–3lb) whole chicken, jointed
25g (¾oz) butter
25ml (¾fl oz) olive oil
1kg (2lb 3oz) potatoes, cut into wedges
1 garlic clove, chopped
1 sprig of rosemary
salt and pepper

For the aïoli
1 batch Homemade Mayonnaise (page 44)
4 quarters of poached quinces, drained (page 28)

For the salad
4 tablespoons Simple Vinaigrette (page 148)
1 teaspoon mustard
100g (3½oz) watercress

Preheat the oven to 180°C/350°F/gas mark 4. Allow the chicken to come to room temperature and then season each piece with salt and pepper. Leave for 15 minutes. Select a large, lidded cast-iron casserole, then melt the butter and oil over a medium heat. Once the butter begins to sizzle, place the chicken pieces, skin side down, into the casserole. Cook until the skin turns golden brown, then transfer the chicken to a plate. Add the potatoes to the casserole, letting them sizzle in the chicken fat, and stirring occasionally so they cook evenly. Stir in the chopped garlic and rosemary, then lay the chicken on top of the potatoes, skin side up, and slide the casserole into the oven.

Cook for 20 minutes then increase the heat to 200°C/400°F/gas mark 6, and cook for an additional 10 minutes. To check the chicken is done, pierce the thickest part of the chicken with a knife. The juices should run clear. Transfer the chicken to a plate and allow it to rest in a warm spot. Stir the potatoes in the juices, then return them to the oven for 10 minutes, or until golden and crisp.

Meanwhile prepare the quince aïoli and watercress salad. Remove the core from the poached quince then place it into a blender with the mayonnaise and blitz until smooth. To make the salad, combine the vinaigrette with the mustard and whisk together. Place the watercress into a bowl and gently toss in the vinaigrette. Taste and adjust with salt and pepper.

When the potatoes are golden and crispy, remove them from the oven. Serve the roasted chicken and potatoes alongside the quince aïoli and mustardy watercress salad.

Pome Fruit

Quince and Calvados Sorbet

This sorbet is astonishingly creamy despite the absence of dairy. It is not only an excellent way to enjoy the pure flavour of quince, but it also allows you to utilize any leftover poached quinces (page 28). I like the subtle hit of heat from the Calvados, but feel free to omit it for a sorbet that is alcohol-free.

SERVES 8–10

2–3 whole quinces

500g (1lb 2oz) Poached Quinces (page 28), cores removed

200ml (7fl oz) of the quince poaching liquid, plus extra

100ml (3½fl oz) Calvados, plus extra to taste

juice of ½ orange

sugar, to taste (optional)

Peel and chop the whole quinces into small pieces, then place into a small saucepan with 300ml (10fl oz) of water. Cover tightly with a lid and put over a high heat. Cook until the quinces begin to steam and fall apart, then reduce the heat and continue to cook with the lid on until the quinces are completely broken down, stirring occasionally to prevent the bottom from burning. Remove from the heat and pass through a large holed colander or food mill, then set the pulp aside.

Once the quince purée has cooled to room temperature, transfer it to a blender. Add the poached quinces, the poaching liquid, Calvados and orange juice. Blend until smooth. If the purée is too thick to blend, gradually add more quince liquid to achieve a smoother consistency. (Please note that this sorbet base will have a thick texture, similar to crème fraîche. Don't worry if it's not pourable; the richness of this thick texture contributes to the luscious and creamy consistency of the sorbet.) Pause the blender and taste the sorbet base. Add more Calvados or a sprinkle of sugar if desired. Spoon the mixture into an ice-cream maker and churn following the manufacturer's instructions. Transfer the churned sorbet to a container and place it in the freezer.

Serving suggestions: Serve with fresh raspberries or blackberries. Or enjoy it with the Almond Cake (page 175) or Almond Meringues (page 116).

DRIED FRUIT

CURRANT, PRUNE, SULTANA, RAISIN

The concentrated sweetness of dried fruits lends a distinct flavour to many dishes synonymous with the colder months. Historically, preserving the bounties of summer and autumn was crucial for enduring the barren winter. Cooking with dried fruit in the colder months, once born out of necessity, has developed into a cultural tradition. While modern storage and transportation methods grant us access to a diverse array of fruits even in winter, incorporating dried fruit, such as currants in mincemeat, echoes an older way of cooking. Beyond traditional winter fare, dried fruits are delicious when tossed through a bright crunchy salad, used in a Neapolitan-inspired flatbread, or preserved in spirits and swirled into ice cream.

DRIED FRUIT PAIRINGS

NUTS	*Almond, chestnut, hazelnut, pecan, pine nut, pistachio, walnut*
FLOWERS, LEAVES AND HERBS	*Bay leaf, rosemary, sage, thyme*
SPICES	*Allspice, anise, black pepper, cardamom, cinnamon, clove, ginger, nutmeg, saffron*
FRUITS	*Apple, kumquat, orange, pear, persimmon, quince*
VEGETABLES	*Broccoli, carrot, cauliflower, chicory, escarole, onion, parsnip, sweet potato, winter squash*
FLOURS	*Plain, polenta, rye, semolina, spelt*
WINES AND SPIRITS	*port, red wine, Sauternes, Vin Santo, Armagnac, bourbon, brandy, Grand Marnier, rum, Scotch, spiced rum, whisky,*
DAIRY, MEAT AND FISH	*Cheddar, Gruyère, Roquefort, beef, chicken, lamb, pâté, pork, terrine, quail, fish (especially sardines), shellfish*
OTHER FLAVOURS	*Brown sugar, black tea, caramel, coffee, chocolate, honey*

FAVOURITE COMBINATIONS WITH DRIED FRUITS

CURRANT • ESCAROLE • PINE NUT | CURRANT • NUTMEG • ORANGE | DATE • ALMOND • SPELT
DATE • CARROT • RADICCHIO | DATE • ORANGE BLOSSOM • BROWN BUTTER
PRUNE • APPLE • ARMAGNAC | PRUNE • WHISKY • CHOCOLATE | RAISIN • SARDINE • SAFFRON
SULTANA • ONION • VINEGAR | SULTANA • PEAR • BRANDY
SULTANA • VIN SANTO • ROQUEFORT

Mincemeat

The quality of your mincemeat largely depends on the ingredients you choose. I suggest investing in the best dried fruit your budget allows. Personally, I indulge in buying Amarena cherries and Agen prunes. Ensure that the nuts and spices are fresh, and select a brandy that you would savour on its own. Since December tends to sneak up on us, I usually prepare this during a quiet moment in late September, which allows the mincemeat time to meld and mellow. If the quantity is more than you plan to use, simply halve the recipe, or gift it at the start of December.

MAKES ABOUT 2.5KG (5½LB) MINCEMEAT (5 x 500G/1LB 2OZ JARS)

350g (12oz) prunes, stoned and finely chopped
350g (12oz) raisins
350g (12oz) currants
175g (6oz) dried sour cherries, chopped
350g (12oz) Candied Citrus Peel (page 54), chopped
125g (4½oz) whole almonds, finely chopped
2 cooking apples
450g (1lb) muscovado sugar, or dark brown sugar
2 teaspoons freshly grated nutmeg
1 teaspoon ground cinnamon
½ teaspoon ground ginger
¼ teaspoon ground coriander
¼ teaspoon ground pepper
½ teaspoon salt
zest and juice of 1 lemon
zest and juice of 1 orange
125ml (4fl oz) brandy
100g (3½oz) unsalted butter, melted

Place the first six ingredients into a large bowl. Grate the apples and their skins over the dried fruit, leaving behind the cores and stems to discard. Combine the muscovado sugar, spices, salt and citrus juice with their zest in another bowl. Mix together, then add the brandy and melted butter. Drizzle the wet ingredients over the dried fruit and using your hands, or a wooden spoon and a lot of elbow grease, stir until all the fruit is coated and the mixture looks well integrated.

Place into a large container and store in a dark, cool place. Stir every day for one week, then transfer to glass jars and store until you are ready to use, or for up to 6 months. If you wish to store the mincemeat for longer, consider sterilizing the jars (see Notes on Making Jam, page 107).

Flatbread with Potato, Escarole, Currants and Pine Nuts

This flatbread is inspired by the Neapolitan *pizza di scarola*, which is more like a pie. Escarole is a leafy, slightly bitter chicory commonly used in Italian cuisine. When cooked, its broad green leaves become tender and flavourful. I prefer the pronounced burst of flavour from the currants, but you can substitute raisins if you wish.

SERVES 6–8

1 quantity Schiacciata Dough (page 151), omitting the honey

plain flour, for dusting

4–5 new potatoes

2 heads of escarole

olive oil

2 garlic cloves

4 anchovy fillets

60g (2¼oz) dried currants, softened in boiling water for 5 minutes

60g (2¼oz) green olives, pitted and halved

¼ teaspoon chilli flakes

60g (2¼oz) pine nuts

salt and pepper

70g (2½oz) Pecorino Romano cheese, to serve

Make the dough a day in advance and refrigerate it overnight. The following day, preheat the oven to 220°C/425°F/gas mark 7 and place a baking stone or inverted baking tray on the middle shelf of the oven. Take another baking tray and brush the bottom generously with olive oil. Remove the dough from the refrigerator and carefully turn the dough onto the tray. Drizzle the top with more oil, then use the tips of your fingers to stretch the dough to 40cm (16in) long. Cover lightly with a tea towel and leave to prove in a warm place for up to 30 minutes. After proving, the dough should be relaxed and risen slightly.

Put the potatoes into a saucepan, cover to the top with cold water and add a few pinches of salt. Bring to the boil, then reduce the heat slightly and cook until the potatoes are easily pierced with a fork. Remove the potatoes from the water and set aside.

Peel back the leaves of the escarole and rinse under cold water. Transfer to a cutting board and give it a rough chop. Place a frying pan over medium–low heat and warm a couple of tablespoons of olive oil. When the oil is hot, chop the garlic and add it to the pan allowing it to gently sizzle for a minute or two. Add the anchovies and mash them into the oil with the back of a wooden spoon. Drop the sliced escarole into the oil, turning and flipping the leaves to prevent the garlic from burning. Drain the currants and add to the pan along with the olives and chilli flakes. Continue cooking until the escarole is wilted and soft. Scrape everything from the pan onto a plate, taste the escarole and adjust the salt and chilli to your liking.

Slice the potatoes and place them on top of the dough. Scatter with the cooled escarole mixture, evenly distributing the currants and olives. Slide the flatbread tray onto the baking stone and bake for about 7–10 minutes until the dough is puffed and golden and the escarole is lightly charred. Meanwhile, lightly toast the pine nuts in a dry frying pan and transfer to a plate to stop the cooking. When the flatbread is ready, scatter the pine nuts over the top and finish with shavings of Pecorino Romano.

Potato Flatbread with Escarole, Currants and Pine Nuts

Dried Fruit

Carrot and Sultana Salad

Here is a light and vibrant shredded salad. The spices provide a warm backnote, while the chilli and mint keep everything fresh.

SERVES 4 AS A SIDE SALAD, OR 2 FOR A LIGHT LUNCH

350g (12oz) carrots

75g (2½oz) sultanas

⅛ teaspoon ground
   cinnamon

¼ teaspoon ground cumin

1 small garlic clove

2 tablespoons lemon juice

1 tablespoon white wine
   vinegar

3 tablespoons olive oil, plus
   extra for serving

To serve

1 small handful of fresh
   mint leaves

50g (2oz) whole almonds,
   toasted and chopped

1 fresh red chilli, thinly
   sliced

Peel the carrots and use a mandolin to julienne them, or grate on a large box grater into a mixing bowl. Place the sultanas in a heatproof bowl, then pour over enough boiling water to completely submerge them. Set aside.

In a mortar, combine the cinnamon, cumin and garlic with a pinch of salt and pound everything into a smooth paste. Add the lemon juice and vinegar, then slowly incorporate the oil. Pour the dressing over the carrots and gently massage it into the carrots. Drain the sultanas well, removing as much excess water as possible, and add them to the bowl of carrots. Give everything a good toss and set it aside for at least 1 hour for the flavours to meld.

When you're ready to serve, coarsely chop the mint leaves. Add half the mint with the almonds and red chilli to the salad. Give everything another toss to combine the flavours. Taste and adjust the seasoning and acidity to your liking. Transfer the salad to a serving plate and finish with a drizzle of olive oil and the rest of the mint.

Prunes in Armagnac

The prunes from Agen, France are renowned for their exquisitely soft texture and thin delicate skin. They are truly worth seeking out for this recipe. However, any other soft prunes will suffice. A dear friend of mine, JR Ryall, leads the pastry kitchen at Ballymaloe House in Cork, Ireland. He has a fondness for soaking prunes in Irish whiskey, a combination I often indulge in during the winter months when the comforting qualities of a good Irish whiskey are most inviting.

SERVES 4–6

200g (7oz) Agen prunes, stoned (see Note)
350ml (12fl oz) boiling water
150ml (5fl oz) Armagnac

NOTE:
To stone the prunes, use your fingers to locate the pointy tip of the stone. Hold the prune upright and with your thumb on the bottom tip of the stone, push the stone up through the top of the prune. This minimizes tearing and preserves the shape of the original fruit.

Place the prunes into a heatproof bowl and pour over the freshly boiled water until two-thirds of the prunes are submerged. Next, add the Armagnac to generously cover the remaining prunes, keeping in mind the prunes will swell as they soak and poke out of the liquid. Allow the prunes to cool, then cover and leave them to soak overnight at room temperature.

The prunes are ready to use the following day, however they do mellow and deepen with time. If you wish to save them for a later date, place them into the refrigerator where they will keep up to a month and possibly longer.

VARIATIONS

Prunes in Whiskey: Swap the Armagnac for Irish whiskey and proceed with the recipe above.

Prunes in Vin de Pêche: Place the prunes into a pan and cover with vin de pêche (see page 163). Warm over a low heat for about 5 minutes until the vin de pêche begins to steam and the prunes feel hot to touch but remove before the liquid has a chance to boil. Cool off the heat and store in a glass container in the refrigerator.

Dried Fruit

Prunes in Armagnac Caramel

A caramel made with prunes and Armagnac is a simple condiment with limitless possibilities. Pair it with chocolate cake, custard or mousse. Drizzle it over ice cream – be it vanilla or coffee – or crème fraîche. Serve it with oranges or caramelized apples. It's worthwhile to have a small jar of it in your pantry throughout the autumn and winter when other varieties of fruit are scarce.

SERVES 4–6

350g (12oz) caster sugar
2 tablespoons water
100ml (3½fl oz) prune-Armagnac soaking liquid (from the recipe opposite)
pinch of salt
2 teaspoons Armagnac
Armagnac-soaked prunes (from the recipe opposite)

Place the sugar into a heavy-based saucepan along with the water. Stir until the sugar is the consistency of wet sand, then cover with a lid and put over a high heat. Cook until the pan begins to steam, then remove the lid and continue to cook undisturbed until the sugar starts to colour slightly. Gently swirl the pan, then reduce the heat slightly and continue to cook to a rich amber caramel. Remove from the heat and stir in the prune-Armagnac soaking liquid and the salt. Leave to settle for 5 minutes, then transfer to a heatproof container and add the Armagnac. Continue cooling to room temperature. This caramel will keep at room temperature in sterilized jars for at least a month, and possibly longer.

When you are ready to serve, strain the prunes from the liquid and place into a heatproof bowl. Warm the caramel gently to loosen it, then pour it over the prunes.

VARIATION
Prunes in Espresso Caramel: Follow the recipe for making caramel sauce, replacing the 100ml (3½fl oz) of prune-Armagnac soaking liquid with water and the 2 teaspoons of Armagnac with espresso. Add a pinch or two of freshly ground espresso beans to the caramel. Soften the prunes in hot water overnight, then drain well before placing them into the caramel.

Dried Fruit

Fruit Cake Ice Cream

Here is a fun ice cream for the winter months. Inspired by the flavours of a traditional British fruit cake, I often make this ice cream around Christmas to serve with apple tart. However, it is perfectly delicious on its own or next to a plate of Soft Almond Cookies (page 141).

SERVES 8–10

400ml (14fl oz) double
  cream
400ml (14fl oz) whole milk
120g (4¼oz) muscovado
  sugar
1 teaspoon salt
½ cinnamon or cassia stick
¼ teaspoon freshly grated
  nutmeg
zest of 1 clementine or ½
  orange
120g (4¼oz) egg yolks
  (from about 6 eggs)
40g (1½ oz) raisins
40g (1½ oz) currants
25g (1oz) stoned prunes
25g (1oz) dried sour
  cherries
130ml (4fl oz) good-quality
  brandy, plus extra for
  soaking
30g (1oz) Candied Citrus
  Peel (page 54), chopped

Place the double cream, milk, sugar, salt, cinnamon, nutmeg and citrus zest into a heavy, non-reactive saucepan and place over a medium heat. Meanwhile, take two large bowls and place iced water in the largest bowl, nestling the other bowl inside. Sit a fine-mesh sieve over the top bowl and set aside somewhere nearby.

Whisk the yolks in a separate bowl, then wrap a tea towel around the base to stabilize it. Once the milk mixture begins to simmer, gradually add the hot milk to the yolks, whisking constantly as you pour. (If your saucepan is too heavy to hold with one hand, then use a ladle or small cup.) Return the mixture to the pan and reduce to a medium–low heat. Gently cook, stirring constantly, until mixture is thick enough to coat the back of a spoon. Strain through the fine-mesh sieve into the cold bowl over the iced water, then continue to stir the custard to stop the cooking. Pour into a container and chill overnight in the refrigerator.

Place the raisins, currants, prunes and sour cherries into a heatproof bowl, cover half the way up with brandy, then fill the rest of the way with boiling water. Allow to cool, then cover and store at room temperature overnight.

The following day, strain the dried fruit and add the chopped candied peel to the mix. Take the ice-cream base out of the freezer and add the 130ml (4fl oz) brandy. Churn in an ice-cream maker according to the manufacturer's instructions. If it is a top churning machine, then in the last few minutes of freezing, scatter the dried and candied fruit over the top. If not, then transfer the smooth ice cream to a chilled container and stir in the additional ingredients by hand. Cover with a piece of baking parchment and store in the freezer for 4–5 hours until firm.

Index

Acknowledgements

To Joanna Copestick and Izzy Jessop for believing in the vision for this book and allowing me the freedom to pursue it. To everyone at Kyle Books who worked to bring this book together. What a joy to see it take shape.

To my agent Alice Saunders for your guidance and words of encouragement. And to Araminta Whitley for putting me in Alice's path.

I owe so much to the incredible team of people who came together for the photoshoots. To Patricia Niven behind the lens, and Henrietta Clancy in the kitchen. To Lisa Gulick who opened her home and heart to us, and whose generosity and artistic eye is in nearly every photograph. Your friendship means so much. To Dor Harel for your exquisite cooking and lightness of touch. For your great taste in music, your great sense of humour and your loyal friendship. To Rachel Vere for the beautiful props and to Rachel Cross for the design. Thank you all for the unforgettable memories, and for bringing my recipes to life. You are all artists.

To Jane Scotter for providing the most beautiful and flavourful produce and flowers. And thank you most of all for the years of invaluable friendship. For the roast chicken dinners and the tranquil Sunday morning strolls around the farm. For the laughter and tears shared over glasses of wine, and always for your kind words of encouragement.

To everyone at Heckfield Home Farm. Especially Peter Quinon, Samantha de Bank and the Market Garden Team. The farm has never looked more beautiful. To the general Manager of Heckfield Place Hotel, Kevin Brookes, and to Ellen de Jager and Fen of the pastry kitchen.

To Alice Waters, Darina Allen and Mary Jo Thoreson for your guidance and mentorship. To Skye Gyngell for creating such a beautiful restaurant and for the collaboration of a lifetime. Thank you for trusting me to run the pastry section and for pushing me to new creative heights.

Thank you to the farmers and growers who shared their stories and knowledge. To David 'Mas' Masumoto, Jane Scotter, Jake Mann, Mags Coughlan and Asunta and Giovanni Bernabei. Thank you to Sara Levi for translating Italian to English.

To everyone who tested, tasted, supported, encouraged or advised. This includes JR Ryall for lighting the spark. To Katherine Heal, Lloyd Morse, Laura Kerr, Tessa Traeger, Anett Hataloczki-Jona, Hazel Allen, Susan Turnerand Patience Gli.

Thank you to my loving husband, Jim, without whose love and support this book would not exist. Thank you for bouncing the baby while I edited, re-edited and edited once again. You are a wonderful father, partner and human being.

And last but not least, thank you to my beautiful family. To my parents who lead by example. Your steadfast dedication to your work and your family is admirable, and paved the way for me to pen this book. I stand on your shoulders. To my beautiful, intelligent and supportive sisters, Leah and Ilana. Your accomplishments, kindness and love inspire me each and every day. I love you all.